ADVENT/CHRISTMAS

From The Desk Of
Judy Doll

Interpreting the Lessons of the Church Year

Arthur J. Dewey

ADVENT/CHRISTMAS

PROCLAMATION 6 | SERIES B

FORTRESS PRESS | MINNEAPOLIS

proclamation

PROCLAMATION 6
Interpreting the Lessons of the Church Year
Series B, Advent/Christmas

Scripture quotations, unless otherwise indicated, are from the New Revised Standard Version
Bible, copyright © 1989 by the Division of Christian Education of the National Council of
Churches in the U.S.A. and are used by permission.

Cover design: Ellen Maly
Text design: David Lott

The Library of Congress has cataloged the first four volumes of Series A as follows:

Proclamation 6, Series A: interpreting the lessons of the church
  year.
        p.   cm.
      Contents: [1] Advent/Christmas / J. Christiaan Beker — [2]
Epiphany / Susan K. Hedahl — [3] Lent / Peter J. Gomes — [4] Holy
Week / Robin Scroggs.
      ISBN 0-8006-4207-4 (v. 1 : alk. paper) — ISBN 0-8006-4208-2 (v.
2 : alk. paper) — ISBN 0-8006-4209-0 (v. 3 : alk. paper) — ISBN 0-8006-4210-4
(v. 4 : alk. paper).
      1. Bible—Homiletical use. 2. Bible—liturgical lessons,
English.
BS534.5P74   1995
251—dc20   95-4622
                                                            CIP
        Series B:
        Advent/Christmas / Arthur J. Dewey—ISBN 0-8006-4215-5
        Epiphany / Mark Allan Powell—ISBN 0-8006-4216-3
        Lent / James H. Harris, Miles Jerome Jones, and Jerome C. Ross—
              ISBN 0-8006-4217-1
        Holy Week / Philip H. Pfatteicher—ISBN 0-8006-4218-X
        Easter / Beverly R. Gaventa—ISBN 0-8006-4219-8
        Pentecost 1 / Ched Myers—ISBN 0-8006-4220-1
        Pentecost 2 / Richard L. Eslinger—ISBN 0-8006-4221-X
        Pentecost 3 / Laura Lagerquist-Gottwald and Norman K. Gottwald—
              ISBN 0-8006-4222-8

The paper used in this publication meets the minimum requirements of American National
Standard for Information Sciences—Permanence of Paper for Printed Library Materials,
ANSI Z329.48-1948.

Manufactured in the U. S. A.   AF 1-4215

00   99   98   97   96   1   2   3   4   5   6   7   8   9   10

Contents

Introduction

ADVENT

The season of Advent traditionally signals a return to the beginning. Communities of faith start all over, taking up their ancient texts. In the midst of a world where God is rarely felt, we yearn to experience God again, for the first time. So we read and listen to our ancestors in faith. We do this trusting that somehow memory and hope will come alive. Each Sunday challenges us to move from cyclical rehearsal to personal breakthrough.

The readings of Advent in their various ways invite us into the presence of God. As we listen to those voices of old, we make a courageous trek in memory. For memory in faith is not some static repetition; rather, it is an active discovery of the possibilities of hope. Those words, images, scenes, and passages that hallow our past open pathways to the mystery in our midst. Each text invites us to ask: How are we entering into the presence of the Holy One?

The **FIRST SUNDAY IN ADVENT** begins and ends *in medias res*. The passage from Isaiah refuses any false optimism for the modern reader. Rather, the cry for God starts amid the ruins, between broken dreams and shattered reality. The prophet wishes for the God of Israel to break into the desolate situation of human life. Paul continues this refusal to leave the present experience. Relying upon the reality of the Spirit in the lives of the Corinthian community, Paul deepens their vision by suggesting that their present life has a profound future that already has begun to work itself out in their life together. Under the pressure of apocalyptic vertigo, the Gospel reading delivers a homely illustration through the use of parabolic remnants. Attentive listeners are challenged to become mindful servants who can detect the future in the fragments of the present.

The **SECOND SUNDAY IN ADVENT** delivers a surprising corrective to those who would deprive us of hope. The first reading from Isaiah presents a vision unimaginable in the ancient world. A chorus of heavenly voices declares that an exiled people is not doomed to extinction but shall return. Second Peter, responding to the growing skepticism among believers in the early second century, boldly challenges listeners to detect the word of God happening in their midst. Finally, the Markan Gospel selection conveys a collage of dramatic images that work from an ancient repertoire of hope. This momentous beginning attempts to transmit shock waves of God's future into the expectant present.

The embodiment of hope is featured in the readings of the **THIRD SUNDAY IN ADVENT**. The selections from Third Isaiah rehearse what it means for people to have true access to their God. Whether through the priestly image of being reconsecrated or the vision of the peaceable kingdom one can enter into the realm where faith is born and out of which we can live. The lesson from Paul is quite practical, stressing that the life of God is alive in the grass roots of the believing community. Our intimation of hope is played out in our life together. In the Gospel from John we can detect the Johannine community's yearning for genuine experience. The invitation to "come and see" is open to all who would dare to make the trek toward transcendence.

The final, **FOURTH SUNDAY IN ADVENT** lets us in on the divine surprise. Our first reading does not simply provide a model of the faithful leader. Rather, the story declares that the God of Israel is not to be domesticated. Precisely because God is surprisingly faithful the people can hope. Even the words of this passage are pregnant in their unfulfilled aspect. The extended doxology of the second reading for today also suggests a breakthrough. Here the traditions, both old and new, become revelatory for this interpolator of Romans. The surprising plan of God comes to light in Jesus. Lastly, the Lukan text takes us to the very limit of human hope and then dares to ask: What does God have to say? We find that God surprises beyond our expectations and invites us to participate freely in this unfinished adventure.

CHRISTMAS

Hardly nostalgic relics are the readings for the feast of the Nativity and Christmas Day. Although the consumer trend of modern society would bleach these texts of any social impact, a close reading indicates that a critical perspective may well be in order. The readings for Christmas refuse to be confined to an unreal realm. The dramatic insight that the surprising presence of God infiltrates all aspects of our lives is embedded in the depths of the Christmas tradition.

The **NATIVITY**'s first selection from Isaiah 9 should be understood in its original setting. In the midst of the political uncertainty of eighth-century Judah a note of hope was sounded. For Isaiah even the quagmire of politics was open to a theological dimension. The passage from Titus continues in such a political vein. Attempting to make the Christian vision relevant to the concerns of the second century, the unknown author intentionally used the imperial language of the period to focus on the fundamental significance of what God has done for humanity. In the Lukan text we can see how the gauntlet has been thrown down against the imperial story. The golden age has begun, not in Rome, nor announced to the elite. Rather, this unlikely ruler comes to the outcasts in what to the Empire would have been a godforsaken place.

The passages for CHRISTMAS DAY build upon the beachhead of hope. In the first reading from Isaiah one finds a sound and light show, where the future is rehearsed. As the return from exile to Jerusalem is envisioned, one detects the compassionate presence of God breaking out in the midst of seemingly endless despair. The second reading presents a fundamental watershed for humanity. In this opening to Hebrews Jesus has made the exodus into the divine realm; he has journeyed into God. Not only is there an opening for humanity but there is a way through—precisely, through death. Finally, the majestic lines of the Johannine prologue continue this passage of hope. There is a way through—into the very heart of humanity. The divine has decided to pitch its tent and stay. The mystery, ever in our midst, is capable of being experienced by us.

THE SUNDAYS AFTER CHRISTMAS

Although there are more disparate readings for the Sundays after Christmas, one can detect that these Sundays continue the movement into the Presence of the Holy One by concentrating on various aspects of our faith existence.

There are three different texts for the first reading for the FIRST SUNDAY AFTER CHRISTMAS. Beginning with Isa. 45:22-25 we come upon a courageous counterclaim to the worship of the Babylonian god Marduk. In these verses we overhear an exiled voice declaring that a "defeated" God is, in fact, the creative heart of the universe and the ultimate source of justice. Nothing can avoid the presence of this Holy One. In the passage from Isa. 61:10—62:3 we can detect a vision of transformation, both of the city and the people. A utopian vision rises above the debris of Jerusalem. Finally, the passages from Genesis feature the faithful response of Abraham as well as the fulfillment of the divine promise of a son. In this ancient tradition we discern the possibility of going to the very edge of one's life.

The selections for the second reading very much focus on our life in faith. In the Galatian passages Paul argues for the maturity already present within the lives of the communities. For him the dream of authentic human life has already begun with their initial trust in Christ. The portion from Hebrews underscores the reality of faith as the basic substance of human life. Examples are provided to encourage listeners to live without any visible means of support. Finally, the Colossians selection extends the earlier

Pauline insight that the community of faith already lives out of the power and dynamic of the resurrection.

In the selection from Luke we come upon the figures of the *Anawim*, those Israelites who have placed all hope in God. Both Simeon and Anna provide stark examples of fundamental trust. The double oracle of Simeon highlights the universal and the scandalous aspects of that amazing child. How do we answer the riddles asking "What child is this"?

The **FEAST OF THE NAME OF JESUS** follows next in this Christmas season. The first reading features either a reading from Numbers or Exodus. In the Numbers passage we encounter an ancient priestly blessing that delivers the best of God to Israel. Even those today who would understand and live out of this blessing are challenged to recognize the basis of the blessing: the never-ending care of God. The passage from Exodus is probably a revision of an early covenantal tradition. Here the reader is invited to return to that ancient desert campsite in the hope that there still will be words of life for those who seek renewal.

The second reading for this Feast is taken from either Romans, Galatians, or Philippians. In the selection from Romans Paul formally introduces himself and his mission to the Jesus believers of Rome. Within the first seven verses of this letter Paul plays off the imperial theology of the empire with a gospel that proclaims a sovereign who reigns not by power and authority but by vulnerability and weakness. In the Philippian selection we come upon the famous pre-Pauline hymn (vv. 6-11), which Paul has revised to point out that the redeeming movement of Jesus goes right into the heart of human frailty and powerlessness. The human struggle itself becomes the locus of the divine presence. (The Galatian selection has been touched on in last Sunday's remarks.)

Although the final verse of the Gospel (Luke 2:15-21) provides the narrative connection with today's feast, v. 19 may well get to the heart of the matter. For "treasuring and pondering all these words" touches directly on the Lukan sense of discipleship. Indeed, the task of the disciple is to turn over all the words and deeds of Jesus in light of the Spirit of the resurrection. This is based upon the Lukan conviction that the Spirit is not gone but ever churning up the depths of our lives.

The final Sunday of the Christmas Season is the **SECOND SUNDAY AFTER CHRISTMAS**. There are three selections for the first readings. The passage from Jeremiah has a storied history. What once was an oracle of hope to the Northern Kingdom delivered by a youthful Jeremiah has been recast during the Babylonian exile to deliver hope also to the southern tribes. What should not be lost to the modern reader is the fantastic claim: that an exiled people should have the unheard of hope not only to survive but to return to their homeland. The alternative reading from Sirach demonstrates the resiliency of a thinker who refuses to give up on his traditions while at the same time not denying the intrusions of a different culture. Here the creation story is recast in the conviction that existence is consistent and that life somehow makes ultimate sense. (Isaiah 61:10—62:3 has been noted above in the First Sunday after Christmas.)

The second reading from Ephesians features a wonderful display of theological confidence. Both the extended benediction and the subsequent thanksgiving give the listener the startling impression that a fundamental plan for the universe exists and is accessible to those who believe. Such a vision becomes a remarkable challenge to the modern eye that sees only alienation and fragmentation.

The final reading from Matthew is a history of Israel in miniature. The exile and return of Jesus from Egypt recapitulates the broader story of his people. Such a passage can bring us up short today. How seriously do we read the story of Jesus in solidarity with his people? Have we learned anything from the Shoah as we reread this tale of getting out of harm's way in the nick of time? (The other selection, John 1:1-18, has been noted on Christmas Day.)

First Sunday in Advent

Lectionary	First Lesson	Psalm	Second Lesson	Gospel
Revised Common	Isa. 64:1-9	Ps. 80:1-7, 17-19	I Cor. 1:3-9	Mark 13:24-37
Episcopal (BCP)	Isa 64:1-9a	Ps. 80:1-7	I Cor. 1:1-9	Mark 13:(24-32) 33-37
Roman Catholic	Isa. 63:16b-17, 19b; 64:2b-7	Ps. 80:2-3, 15-16, 18-19	I Cor. 1:3-9	Mark 13:33-37
Lutheran (LBW)	Isa. 63:16b-17; 64:1-8	Ps. 80:1-7, 17-19	I Cor. 1:3-9	Mark 13:33-37 or Mark 11:1-10

FIRST LESSON: ISAIAH 63:16b—64:9

Our liturgical year begins in devastating fashion. The first lesson for today features an extended outcry from Third Isaiah. Indeed, in our present age, when many are decrying the absence of God in both public and private spheres, when a sense of violation and the ache of meaninglessness attack deep within, the haunting poetry of today's lesson strikes a sadly familiar note.

Isaiah 63:16b—64:9 actually forms most of the second half of a well-crafted lament (63:7—64:12) in Third Isaiah. The eclectic collection of material (chaps. 56–66) called Third Isaiah originated sometime after the edict of Cyrus (538 B.C.E.) and before the rebuilding of the Temple in Jerusalem (515 B.C.E.). Writing in the tradition and momentum of Second Isaiah, the visionary of Third Isaiah delivered his message in Jerusalem to a mixed audience of residents and those who returned from the Babylonian exile. In his own way, the writer of Third Isaiah presented a consistent message of hope. Yahweh will rebuild the community in Zion, so that the divine glory will be revealed. Israel will return to the covenant and await the creative visitation of God. The judgment of God will separate the true Israel from the wicked, that is, those who oppress their neighbors and remain closed to the divine presence.

Yet, in today's reading there appears little note of hope. Coming directly after what functions as the centerpiece of Third Isaiah (chaps. 60–62) where the future glorification of Zion is envisioned, and after a brief poem of divine vengeance (63:1-6), the lament of 63:7—64:12 brings the reader up short. Why was this elaborate poem placed after such visions of utopian delight and victory? Such a juxtaposition probably reflects the historical reality of a people caught between their dreams and shattered reality. This lament echoes through the ruins of a desolate Jerusalem (63:18-19; 64:10-11).

A more detailed reading of this lament reveals an extremely rich texture. In 63:7-14 we have the first half of the lament. Here a case is made through a recital of the deeds that brought Israel into existence. Verse 7 presents a prefatory remark to what follows. In vv. 8-14 the exodus ordeal is recounted. A number of points should be noted. First, emphasis is placed upon the active presence of God ("no messenger or angel but his presence that saved them" (63:9 NRSV). Second, the legendary rebellion in the desert (cf. Psalm 106) has been inserted, thereby echoing the preexilic situation. Third, Moses is remembered as using indirect questions to reproach the "One who brought the people out of the sea" (cf. vv.11b-12b). The first part concludes with the affirmation that God delivered the people.

The lament takes a decided turn in 63:15. Until that verse the direct relationship of Yahweh with the people was only suggested at the beginning (v. 7, "all that the LORD has done for us") and at the end of the recital (v. 14, "Thus you led your people"). The past recounting, however, becomes the basis for 63:15—64:12. Now present demands and questions flood the floor. The poet calls on Yahweh to "look down from heaven and see" (63:15). Then, following the figure of Moses, he asks where is the evidence of God's passion for the people. He continues by demanding to know why the people have lost their fear of God (63:17). In a most moving verse he acknowledges God as "father," the "redeemer from of old," in contrast to the father figures of Abraham and Israel who have come and gone (63:16). The reproaches of vv. 17-19 attempt to play to the honor of the divine patron.

The poet then expresses a most ardent wish for Yahweh to break into the peoples' lives and desolate condition. Drawing on the Exodus imagery of a seismic theophany (64:1, 3; Exod. 19:16-18), the sad singer touches the core of the relationship of Yahweh with the people. Despite the situation that all are mortal, fallible, and alienated, the poet can still call out to a God who is their parent, who remembers them beyond their failure. In fact, in a most telling verse we hear: "No eye has seen any God besides you, who works for those who wait for him. You meet those who gladly do right. . ." (64:4b-5a). Here in the midst of absence and devastation there is an intimation of presence. The people are being tutored in waiting for God. But it is no futile "waiting for Godot." On the contrary, "those who do right" are on the verge of meeting the One who "tears open the heavens and comes down." Within the complaints resounding through the debris of a fractured past, comes a hint as subtle as a people's memory.

The subtle clues of this lament should not be lost on the modern listener. We must remember that this piece is primarily a song which expresses the heart of a people. In fact, it was intended to reach the heart of God

(63:15). Thus, our initial questions perhaps should come from the echoes of this song within our experience and that of our communities. As a lament, this lesson instructs us to see that our feelings, disappointments, memories, and emptiness become a way to mystery. Indeed, in acknowledging and creatively attending to those seismic shocks to our psyches and societies, we may well be on the verge of a breakthrough into God.

SECOND LESSON: I CORINTHIANS 1:1-9

The second lesson comes from the beginning of Paul's First Letter to the Corinthians. Writing in either 53 or 54 C.E. from Ephesus, Paul attempted to advise the Corinthian congregation on a number of issues. Evidently the Corinthian community had responded to the original preaching of Paul with gusto and had confirmed his message with their own diversified experience of the Spirit. From their letter to him (1 Cor. 7:1) and from the report of Chloe's people (1 Cor. 1:11), however, Paul came to understand that the initial trends of enthusiasm had generated an internal elitism, which manifested itself in their worship and social organization. From Paul's perspective the heart of the Corinthian problem rested in the phenomenon of factionalism and the lack of communal identity.

Working indirectly from the letter itself, the reader can detect what might well have been the position of the Corinthians. Many of the Corinthians thought of themselves as mature, Spirit-filled individuals, who exercised their freedom in the name of the Lord Jesus. All things, therefore, were lawful for those who had passed beyond material and bodily constraints and had already experienced the resurrection in saving knowledge. It is crucial to recognize that it was the community's genuine experience of the Spirit which served as the basis of their individualistic interpretation. Certainly Paul does not deny their experience of the Spirit. What he tries to do throughout the letter is to persuade his listeners to see that the lack of a collective identity is their fundamental problem and that their fondness for religious fulfillment (even among the weak) in preference to the upbuilding of the community breaks the spiritual body asunder. In contrast to an elitism of the spiritually fulfilled individual, Paul presents a democratized version of life together in the Spirit. If one wants to discern the true face of wisdom, then find it in exposure to the weakness of the cross of Jesus and in solidarity with the "weak" members of the community. In brief, the Corinthians had not yet comprehended the social reality of what it means to be "spiritual" and "in Christ."

From the outset of the letter Paul discloses his concern. While today's lesson provides us with just the tip of the iceberg, it nevertheless anticipates the issues noted above. Moreover, both form and rhetorical criticism can aid the modern reader in determining Paul's persuasive intent. Verses 1-3, for example, serve as the epistolary prescript of the letter, while vv. 4-9 function as the formal opening of his address to the Corinthian community.

The prescript of an ancient letter contains three basic elements: the superscription (the sender's name), the adscription (addressees), and the salutation (greetings). It is well known that Paul usually exploits this simple literary formula to send particular signals. Thus, in giving his title (and thereby indicating his authority to give advice), Paul underlines the divine origin of his calling. Additionally, his mention of the comrade Sosthenes intimates the social connection that will shortly be emphasized. Paul then goes on to address the assembly (*ekklesia*) in Corinth. Only after stressing the unity of the community by this politically charged word does he describe the individuals as "made holy [NRSV: sanctified] in Christ Jesus." He deliberately links the Corinthian "saints" with "all who everywhere invoke the name of the Lord Jesus Christ." Just as Roman citizens could universally invoke the name of Caesar as their patron, so here Paul points to a radically competitive patronage system. In fact, the very greetings Paul sends are precisely the divine benefits of "peace and prosperity."

The rhetorical opening of Paul's advice to the Corinthians begins in earnest in vv. 4-9. Here Paul attempts to gain the attention, good will, and receptivity of his audience in order to orient them to the argument that is to come. By delivering words of praise ("in every way you have been enriched in him"), he craftily prepares them for the critical advice that will follow. In fact, such words of praise are couched in a public prayer of thanksgiving, whereby Paul acknowledges the benefit (*charis*) given to them by God in Christ Jesus. He elaborates on this by specifying that they have been endowed with every eloquence and enlightenment (v. 5), that the "witness of Christ" has been publically confirmed in them (v. 6). Yet, the unabashed focus on the present good fortune of the community changes abruptly with the introduction of a future note ("while you eagerly await the breakthrough of our Lord Jesus Christ," v. 7b). Paul interjects the vision of the final day when the Corinthians will stand "blameless" due to Christ Jesus (v. 8). The final verse is more of an exclamation, testifying to the trustworthiness of God, who called the Corinthians into the fellowship of the divine Son (v. 9).

Consider how, in the short space of an introductory prayer, Paul tries not only to capture the imagination of his audience but also to establish a new perspective. He suggests to the community that they should not live from the established patterns of present fulfillment. Rather, he attempts to move them to discern that they are living actually out of the future, God's future. Furthermore, this future with God—that has begun in them—is inherently social. The fellowship of Jesus Christ establishes both the particular community in Corinth and the universal community throughout the civilized world. To dwell excessively upon one's individual rights and benefits at the expense of the fellowship thus misses the radical breakthrough in Christ.

Such rhetorical strategy should not be lost on the modern Bible reader. At this time of the liturgical year we are asked to consider our future with God. How often we overlook the wisdom of our older brother Paul. Do we understand that the spiritual life is not simply an individual quest but a communal discovery? Can our churches entertain such troubling possibilities? Do we allow other voices to disturb us from our search for fulfillment and meaning? Are we able to be surprised that we live not from ourselves but out of the very life of God?

GOSPEL: MARK 13:24-37

The Gospel of Mark was written at a critical time. The Temple had fallen, Jerusalem had been taken, and hundreds of thousands of Jews had lost their lives. Crucified bodies hung before the eyes and memories of the survivors. What was a Jewish sect to make of this trauma? How to make sense of the end of what was known and familiar? A major part of understanding the Markan response to these happenings can be found in today's reading. The Markan community saw such events as the beginning of the final drama of time and space and wished to orient themselves in light of that very uncertain future. How does one live in discipleship during a time of perceived social and political upheaval? To determine the Markan response let us consider the imaginative language of what is called the Markan Apocalypse (chap. 13).

Apocalyptic language was first used by Jews in the second century B.C.E. to deal with the political, economic, and religious oppression by their Syrian overlords. Instead of giving in to the cultural and political pressures of the day, these Judean visionaries attempted to put everything, including human history, into proper perspective. Indeed, the basic question of whether God is just to the suffering innocent was fundamental to their considerations. Thus, the appropriation of such imagery by the writer of Mark (vv. 24-27) fits in quite well with the basic problems of orientation of the Markan community. Such language hints of the vertigo experienced by the community. The words reflect the sense of historical uncertainty and pressure.

The apocalyptic material is not the only aspect of this passage. In vv. 28-29 we see a commonplace proverb being set within this final vision, while in vv. 30-31 we have prophetic utterances (cf. Mark 9:1) from pre-Markan traditions. Verse 32 is especially curious. In many apocalyptic passages we have the seer or visionary telling a select group of disciples what the end times will be like. Through sometimes rather bizarre symbolism the visionary communicates the "timetable" of the last days. In Mark 13, however, there is a decided difficulty with Jesus as seer. Instead of finally answering the question (13:4) of the disciples (who represent the later Markan community), Jesus admits that he does not know! Despite the tension of the period in which they lived the Markan community would have been unable to use Jesus as some comfortable way out. No insurance policy or safety net has been provided. Instead, the entire thirteenth chapter of Mark works to encourage those who were in the midst of a variety of trials. It was for the Markan community to make sense of the coming situation by employing their wisdom, imagination, and tradition.

The final exhortation (vv. 33-37) to the Markan community may well include fragments of an earlier parable (vv. 34, 35, 36). The story of a man going on a trip and putting his slaves in charge of his house has been turned by Mark into an illustration for the Markan community. We can easily see this by the intrusion of the second person plural (vv. 35, 36) into the story, linking up with the framing exhortations in vv. 33 and 37. Here we have an example of how an earlier tradition is revised.

It is quite interesting to note that while the rest of Mark 13 is fraught with heavy apocalyptic imagery, the final illustration comes from a pedestrian situation. A return of the "lord of the manor" is not in the same league as falling stars, earthquakes, and international war. Is there anything significant to this? The genius in applying such a homely illustration is that the original listeners would easily identify with that experience. There is something more, however. The listeners, in identifying with the slaves in charge of the house, would understand their roles as responsible actors in this final apocalyptic drama. The future is indeed on its way, but they now have a part in it. Passivity gives way to readiness and response.

We should note that this passage as well as a number of other apocalyptic pieces will be used more and more frequently as we approach the year 2000. Again much ink will be spilt and hard disks filled to capacity over speculation concerning the end times. Elaborate calculations and intricate schemes will be constructed between the Bible and the daily news. Unfortunately, all such efforts overlook the experience and suggestions of the early Jesus believers. People inclined to an uncritical reading should take

Mark 13:32 more seriously. If the Markan Jesus is ignorant of the end, what justifies their modern speculations? Further, such simplistic interpretations actually miss the deeper possibilities of this material. For this passage points to a basic attitude on the part of the believer. This passage calls for a special alertness that permeates one's entire life. Responsibility and readiness are understood as intrinsic to the life of faith. It is not a call to anxiety, nor a call to mindlessness. Rather, it is a challenge to critical adventure. Be on the alert because there is something real here. Life is in movement, the game's afoot! We are not victims to the givens of our culture; instead, we are responsible servants of the future.

Do we trust that there is One who wakes us from our imaginative and social stupor? We overlook the One who encourages—at our peril. Are we able to imagine something beyond the predictable headlines of our day? Are we able to serve one another in the household of this planet? Have we ever experienced that we can be more alive than our society would allow us to believe?

Second Sunday in Advent

Lectionary	First Lesson	Psalm	Second Lesson	Gospel
Revised Common	Isa 40:1-11	Ps. 85:1-2, 8-13	2 Peter 3:8-15a	Mark 1:1-8
Episcopal (BCP)	Isa 40:1-11	Ps. 85:7-13	2 Peter 3:8-15a, 18	Mark 1:1-8
Roman Catholic	Isa 40:1-5, 9-11	Ps. 85:8-14	2 Peter 3:8-14	Mark 1:1-8
Lutheran (LBW)	Isa 40:1-11	Psalm 85	2 Peter 3:8-14	Mark 1:1-8

FIRST LESSON: ISAIAH 40:1-11

Perhaps the most appropriate commentary for this famous passage from Second Isaiah is the opening of Handel's *Messiah*. For those untold numbers who have participated in this oratorio there is the recognition along a number of human registers of a hope that is uttered finally and joyfully proclaimed.

Today's passage, delivered to the exiled Jewish community languishing in a foreign land, functions as the inaugural oracle for Second Isaiah (Isaiah 40–55). This collection of material was produced during the 540s B.C.E. when Cyrus, king of Persia, was threatening the neo-Babylonian Empire. The author of Second Isaiah preached the restoration of the people. Just as Isaiah of Jerusalem saw the Assyrian king as an instrument of Israel's punishment (10:5-19) so now the prophet of Second Isaiah considered the Persian king as the instrument of restoration (44:24—45:13). Taking over the Exodus-Conquest tradition (cf. Hosea 2; Ezekiel 20), he imagined the leaving of Babylon and the return to Zion as a renewal of the original exodus from Egypt and conquest of Canaan. Only the act of a supreme God could bring about the creation of a new society for an exiled people, thwarted from returning home by both their captors and the intervening desert. Indeed, what he envisioned was for that time unimaginable: a defeated and exiled people coming home instead of fading into the sands of history.

Just as its counterpart in Isaiah 6, the scene for this passage begins in the heavenly court. The divine decision has already been reached and is now communicated through various heavenly voices. The first anonymous voice (vv. 1-2) utters the opening note of compassion, as well as decreeing that the time of Israel's exile is over (reversing the sentence of Isa. 6:11-12). A second unknown heavenly courtier commands the assembly to build a highway through the impassable desert separating Babylon from Palestine. The "highway" has a number of possible associations. Recalling the exodus from Egypt and conquest of Canaan, it also keeps alive the memory of the triumphant procession of God's people after that victory (Exod. 15:13-18). It may also play off the grand processions of the Babylonian feasts. In any event, the creation of such a highway would be a miraculous event, possible only through divine intervention.

In vv. 6-8 the heavenly decree continues to move out. A third anonymous voice speaks to the prophet who, like Isaiah of Jerusalem, is told to announce what he has seen and heard to people of God. As representative of the people the prophet expresses the community's exhaustion and does so in a traditional lament (vv. 6c-7; cf. Pss. 90:5-6; 103:15-16). There may also be some allusion to the notion that only a genuine prophet can attend a divine assembly (cf. Jer. 23:18). However, the courtier responds that although the people might fade God's word can revive them (v. 8). Then either another anonymous voice or the prophet commands Jerusalem, personified as mother and queen, to go to a high (probably cosmic) mountain and announce the coming of Yahweh to cities of Judah (vv. 9-11). And, although powerful (v. 10), God will come also as a compassionate king (v. 11; shepherd is a traditional designation for king).

There is much to learned from this prophetic chorus. This opening piece is nothing less than a percussive onslaught against the political and theological reality of the late sixth century B.C.E. Against what would seem to be the insurmountable odds of extinction, a Jewish voice counters with the hope not only to return but to do so in miraculous fashion. This vision becomes even more preposterous when one considers the untold numbers of ancient peoples who were driven into exile, never to be heard from again. Yet, here the word returns. It comes back in resounding fashion, from the heavenly assembly, through the deserts of the Middle East, even to the hills and cities of Judah. The exodus begins again because the people understand at last that God forever creates and refuses to forget God's own.

Are we able today to hear such spine-tingling sounds? Can we bear the joy that God wants to share with us? Do we see that hope does not die but only that our imaginations fail? Are we so overcome with the so-called realities of our age that we cannot detect any hints to the contrary? Do we recognize that the human wish to return home is already being answered? Do we hear those hopeful sounds promising that the alienation of our lives will be utterly transformed?

SECOND LESSON: 2 PETER 3:8-18

Our second lesson comes from one of the more obscure writings of the New Testament. 2 Peter is a pseudonymous letter dated no earlier than the first quarter of the second century. It was apparently written to reiterate the hope for the coming of the Lord in the face of growing skepticism and to stand firm against those who no longer held to this expectation.

From a close reading of the entire letter one can learn that times have certainly changed. The first generations of the Jesus believers have passed away along with the intensity of their eschatological vision. Other teachers have emerged, criticizing such future scenarios. They may well have stressed the need to focus on the saving knowledge ("gnosis") found in the present as well as the eventual translation to the heavenly realm. To be concerned about a material conclusion to the cosmos may well have been seen as part of the collusion with this benighted world. We also learn that the writings of Paul have been collected as "scripture," that there are other "twisted" interpretations of the Pauline corpus. Could this be a response to the Marcionite appropriation and arrangement of the letters of Paul? Or, is that an allusion to other gnostic interpreters who sought the pneumatic understanding of Paul's writings?

In countering these issues, the writer of 2 Peter has chosen to craft the letter in the form of a testament. The testament genre comes from the Jewish literary tradition (Genesis 49; *The Testaments of the Twelve Patriarchs*). According to the format the patriarch, approaching death, calls his family together to recount his life, predict what will happen, and warn and exhort his survivors. Thus, the figure of Peter, alluding to his death (1:14), makes provision for his teaching to be remembered (1:14; 3:1) and predicts the coming of false teachers after his demise (3:3). The writer of 2 Peter adds a number of apologetic passages (1:16-21; 2:3b-10a; 3:5-10) along with two extended exhortations (2:10b-22; 3:1-16).

Today's selection (2 Pet. 3:8-18) needs some context. After an extensive critique of the opposition (2:10b-22), the writer returns to the focus of concern: his audience and their understanding of the future. From 3:1-2 it would appear that there were certain canonical writings (including 1 Peter?) which they were to remember. He then anticipates the opposition's skepticism of the coming of the Lord (3:3-4). He explains that their static view of history ignores the dynamic history created by God's word. History has three ages, with the cataclysms of water and fire separating the times. It is at this point our lesson begins. The writer presents an ingenious response to the skeptics. Not only is God's time different from human conception but the problem of the delay of the parousia becomes an opportunity for salvation (3:8-9). Divine patience, not divine tardiness, is the point. Then, employing apocalyptic imagery common to the Synoptics (Matt. 24:42; Luke 12:39) and 1 Thess. 5:2, he joins the traditional Jewish vision of the Day of the Lord with the common Greek assumption of the destruction of the earth by fire (v. 10).

Upon this revision of eschatological thinking, the writer then exhorts his listeners to choose "what sort of persons they ought to be." Here the writer rather creatively persuades his listeners to live a life of holiness in the midst of the corruption of this world. A life of patience, peace, and holiness becomes the "entry into the eternal kingdom" (1:11), as the people learn to become participants in the divine nature (1:4). He then brings in the wisdom from their older brother Paul, despite the difficulty of his letters and the way some people twist them (3:16). After a final warning about "lawless" teachers, and a last exhortation to grow in the "knowledge" of the Lord, there is a simple doxology "both now and to the day of eternity" (3:18).

The creative attempt of this second-century author should not be overlooked. Here we have an attempt both to live out of the long awaited future and to maintain fidelity to the ancestors in faith who delivered such a future. The writer tried to make sense of his tradition for changing circumstances. However, the modern interpreter may well miss this point if only a simplistic interpretation is made. Simply repeating the labels, the cautions, and the pious phrases of a past age will not faithfully convey the momentum of this text. For the writer of 2 Peter directly asks us: What future do you truly believe in? Do you detect God's word in what is happening around you? What sort of persons do you want to be? Can you find in your life access to the presence of God?

GOSPEL: MARK 1:1-8

In a fitting sequel to last Sunday's Gospel, the Markan scene of John's proclamation of repentance embodies well the sense of alertness and preparation already encouraged in last week's reading. What appears to be a simple introductory scene, however, takes on the aspect of a complicated drama for the ancient and modern audiences.

First, Mark alerts the listener to the fact that he is using earlier traditions. His citation (allegedly only from Isaiah in vv. 2-3) forms the basis of his rhetorical and dramatic argument. More precisely, Mark is not simply quoting Isaiah in vv. 2 and 3. "I send my messenger before you" comes either from Exod. 23:20 or from Mal. 3:1 (which would include "to prepare your way"). Only v. 3 is taken from Isa. 40:3. Now the original sense is changed by Mark. "A herald's voice cries" is actually the introduction to "In the desert make ready. . . ." Mark has also changed "path of our God" to "his path." In v. 2, Malachi's "before me" has been changed to "before you." What is going on here? Is it merely a word game? On the contrary, the passage is the result of serious scribal sifting of Scripture based upon the assumption that God's word will come to pass. The verses have been creatively assembled, perhaps through the catchwords "way of the Lord," in an effort to understand the role John played in relation to Jesus. This effort was probably warranted because the followers of John claimed (some for over three hundred years) that he, not Jesus, was to announce the advent of God. Indeed, if one were to read the quotations from the various sources without their having been touched up, John would appear to be the herald of the end time. Yet the Jesus believers saw John as Elijah *redivivus*, who was to come just before the Messiah. Instead of seeing John as the final messenger of God, the Jesus believers understood him as the penultimate witness; Jesus was their Messiah.

By placing the quotation from Scripture before the story of the Baptizer, Mark demonstrates how Scripture is fulfilled by John's preaching of repentance. Even his clothing becomes a clue to the Elijah theme (see Zech. 13:4; 2 Kings 1:8). The presence of Elijah raises a deeper issue of this passage. Elijah was to return at the end of time. Indeed, the last words of today's Gospel, "he will baptize you with Holy Spirit," cause us to think of Judgment Day. The "baptism of repentance" was likely seen as a seal of protection for all those who turn from their sins in order to avoid the wrath to come. This entire passage is radical in its perspective. The time for God's visitation is near. The "One more powerful" is coming. The lingering question for the tradition is the identity of the "One who comes."

Let us now address the final compositional level of the material in order to ask what meaning this has for us today. We have noted that the writer of Mark has taken traditions both recent and old to create a utopian vision. It is also important to recognize that this scene comes not from the time of John the Baptizer but from that of the later Markan community. The Jewish hope for an end time that begins with the return of Israel to God is indicated by the positive response by both town and country to the message of John. The collage of prophetic texts (vv. 2-3) and the investing of John as Elijah *redivivus* (v. 6) support this artistic composition. In other words, the scene is set not simply for the entrance of Jesus (v. 9) but especially for the expectations of the audience. The writer draws upon images that stir the fires of human hope. Indeed, this scene conveys a revolutionary sense when we juxtapose it with what was said in last Sunday's commentary. To evoke such a scene before a community that was traumatized by the fall of the Temple and the deaths of thousands of Jews is an attempt to begin again, to find renewal now in the story of Jesus.

It may well be that this angle of interpretation can speak to us today. It is not a matter of simply noting that Mark revised earlier traditions. Rather, it is the fact that the writer did make a creative effort which can provoke us today. The use of this composition for the first-century community meant that they could interpret their traumatic experience in a different direction. The writer played upon their repertoire of hopes in getting them to identify with the figure of John. For they were called to see that just as John proclaimed this new era, and just as Jesus did, so they, too, were to take an active part in the drama of discipleship.

The task for the modern preacher and community is to continue this direction of hope. What is our repertoire of desires? Do we even dare compose a scene embodying our hope? Yet, how can we speak of renewal or change of heart unless we begin to imagine such possibilities? In other words, how can we turn what is on the surface a cyclical event into a personal breakthrough? How can we move from a nostalgic image of Christian beginnings to a genuine starting point? Does not the absent figure of Jesus give us a clue? All the images and citations receive their perspective from this absent focal point. What would happen if we were to allow our fundamental hopes to gravitate around this hidden One? We could even bring forward the story from Mark and discern how this would be reconfigured within our emerging composition. John would continue to point the way insofar as we take up the task of faithful enactment.

Another way of putting this is that today's opening passage is suggestive of the entire Gospel of Mark. With the baptism of Jesus, it forms the overture to the Markan drama, for the faithful of the Markan community saw themselves, shortly after the fall of Jerusalem, as being involved in the same pattern of witness as were John and Jesus. The Markan community, too, were to preach the Good News and, most likely, be delivered up. Thus the quote at the beginning had a twofold meaning for them. It charged them to "make ready the way of the Lord," and, by their preaching and suffering, they became "messengers" before the Lord.

Such an understanding turns past into present. The oracle addresses us. We are asked to "make ready." In so doing, we take on the features of the long line of prophetic witnesses. We are challenged, not simply to hear, but to participate in the baptism of God, who turns all time into the Good News of Jesus Christ.

Third Sunday in Advent

Lectionary	First Lesson	Psalm	Second Lesson	Gospel
Revised Common	Isa. 61:1-4, 8-11	Psalm 126 *or* Luke 1:47-55	1 Thess. 5:16-24	John 1:6-8, 19-28
Episcopal (BCP)	Isa. 65:17-25	Psalm 126 *or* Canticle 3 *or* 15	1 Thess. 5:(12-15) 16-28	John 1:6-8, 19-28 *or* John 3:23-30
Roman Catholic	Isa. 61:1-2a, 10-11	Luke 1:46-50, 53-54	1 Thess. 5:16-24	John 1:6-8, 19-28
Lutheran (LBW)	Isa. 61:1-3, 10-11	Luke 1:46b-55	1 Thess. 5:16-24	John 1:6-8, 19-28

FIRST LESSON: ISAIAH 61:1-4, 8-11; 65:17-25

(For more background on Third Isaiah please see the introductory comments for the first lesson of the First Sunday of Advent.)

ISAIAH 61:1-4, 8-11

Our first lesson for today is a genuine dress rehearsal. In this poem we hear through the prophetic voice of Third Isaiah the announcement that the long oppressed people of Israel will put on the priestly insignia and clothing as they rebuild their devastated land. Yahweh's vindication is near as the people will become glorious, receiving what is due them from the nations of the world. The priestly insertion of Exod. 19:6 ("and you shall be to me a kingdom of priests and a holy nation [RSV]) finds an echoing confirmation in this material.

The distinctive voice of Third Isaiah is detected from the outset of the poem. Instead of the "Word of the Lord" coming to a preexilic prophet, the "Spirit of the Lord" comes upon the speaker in the same fashion as in Second Isaiah (42:1; 48:16). He has been "anointed," that is, commissioned to act as a messenger. In preexilic times only priests and kings were anointed (with the sole exception of Elijah). His mission is to announce God's justice to the poor of Israel. Notice that the various terms describing those effected ("oppressed," "brokenhearted," "captives," "prisoners," and "mourners") actually refer to the 'Anawim, the faithful poor who have been deprived of justice. Thus, the poet is speaking on behalf of those who were being neglected in the restored Israel. As to the actual time of vindication, the prophet is somewhat vague. In v. 2 it is the "year" or the "day." In other words, the reversal of the poor people's fortune is near but unspecified.

In v. 3 we find a telling use of imagery. The people will wear a "turban," [NRSV: garland] be anointed with the "oil of gladness" and the "mantle of praise." Such images suggest priestly consecration (Exodus 28–29; Leviti-

25

cus 8). This priestly allusion is continued in vv. 5-7, where the people are not only called "priests" and "ministers" of God, but they receive a double portion of tithes from the nations as recompense for their earlier abasement. Lastly, v. 10 presents the prophet now uttering a priestly song of thanksgiving, clothed with the "garments of salvation" and the "robe of righteousness." He is like a "bridegroom" who "priests it" or "decks himself out" with a turban.

What is the point for employing such priestly imagery? What was the writer of Third Isaiah communicating to the people? What would these words have stirred in the ancient imaginations? The selection of such images would have spoken volumes to the honor of a devastated people. To put on the robes of a once revered priesthood, to recall imaginatively what it means to have access to the divine, to feel empowered once more, with an identity as a people restored and secure—all of this would flood in with such metaphors. Moreover, these images are not reserved for the house of Aaron; rather, they are directed to all those who have been overturned by the exile, including especially the very people now overlooked in the restored Israel.

Indeed, the poem touches on a fundamental discovery from the exilic experience. Despite the ruin of the exile and the rubble of the return, the vision of Third Isaiah reaches the essential reality of the covenant of Yahweh with Israel. In vv. 8-9 we hear from the God who "loves justice," promising vindication and an everlasting covenant for the people. Yahweh's favor of Israel will be known among all the peoples of the world. In brief, God's faithful relationship becomes clear in the moment of havoc and despair. From this understanding of God can the people put on the priestly garments with confidence as they attempt to rebuild their lives and land.

Christians will be reminded of Luke 4:16-20 when reading this passage. But one should not be too eager to make a direct connection. For too hasty a linkage may keep us from hearing a declaration on behalf of the faceless ones ('Anawim). Despite the Christian appropriation of these verses, this utterance is still unfulfilled in the modern world. The question still remains: Do we believe that this is God's good news for us? Are we able to bear the message that the wretched of the earth will wear the clothes of respectability and receive honor from those who oppressed them? Dare we celebrate this vision with anticipatory thanksgiving?

ISAIAH 65:17-25
Another reading for today's second lesson presents a palimpsest of hope. Isaiah 65:17-25 reiterates and expands on the vision of Jerusalem's restoration and glory (Isa. 60:1—62:12). [For more on this material see the com-

ments below on the first lessons of the First and Second Sundays after Christmas.] The divine voice declares the creation of new heavens and a new earth (v. 17). What should be underscored is that this new creation is not simply a physical affair. Rather, this new situation entails a regenerated relationship with the people (vv. 18c, 19b).

A moving vision of what this renewed relationship implies is detailed in vv. 21-23. Certainly for a people who have not long returned from exile pictures of living and enjoying one's home (vv. 21-22), of being confident that one's children will live in peace and away from terror (v. 23), will be quite attractive. Verse 20 appears to be a later addition to this hopeful scenario. However, the image of a healthy, long life is a welcome addition.

Verses 24-25 conclude this positive oracle. In contrast to Isa. 65:1-2, where Yahweh was ready to be sought out but was not, v. 24 reassures the people that God will be there to hear even before they begin to pray. The paradisal images in v. 25a, b are actually a revision of an earlier vision of harmony found in Isa. 11:6, 7, while v. 25d repeats Isa. 11:9. Such images may also play upon the memories of Isa. 2:1-4 and Genesis 2. These natural "surprises" become symbolic of the kind of life that is to be lived by all upon God's holy mountain (cf. Isa. 56:7).

What should not be lost on us is the creative depth of this passage. This text continues to fascinate readers. Not only can scenes of a "peaceable kingdom" be easily sketched out, but the opening words themselves ("I am about to create . . .") suggest the basis of all human creativity and hope. For in this passage images speak to the depths of society and the subconscious. Here the realm of dream and hope appear, where the future is born and out of which we live. These startling images of Third Isaiah are just as challenging today, for they ask whether our communities can be open to the depths of God's creativity. Can we imagine a world where violence is no more, where justice is a matter of fact, and where we can be human to one another?

SECOND LESSON: I THESSALONIANS 5:16-28

The second reading comes from a final exhortation by Paul in his letter to the Thessalonians. Writing most likely from Corinth (50 C.E., Acts 18:5) after receiving a report from Timothy (3:6) that the grass roots community in Thessalonica was growing despite opposition (1:6b), Paul from the outset of the letter encourages the community to continue to act in the way for which they have become famous (1:8), that is, their ever-growing faith, hope, and love. Now the basis for the surprising (even to Paul) growth of the community is also the ground for the community's very existence: the proclamation and reception of the gospel (1:5, 7, 8-9). In regard to both the proclamation and welcome of the word the "handling" of the gospel is inherently personal. In order for the gospel to grow the believers must undertake personal risk (1:6-7).

Significantly, this letter to the Thessalonians never leaves the level of the practical. From the beginning to the end Paul's vision and advice arise from a reflection upon the experience of the community. Furthermore, this aspect of reflection upon communal experience can be expanded if Paul is using his experience from Corinth to aid the Thessalonians in coming to understand their position and role in the gospel proclamation. Paul's mentioning of ecstatic activity could be taken from the pneumatic experience in Corinth. Thus, the exhortations of 5:16-24 are not pious platitudes but wise recommendations reached from genuine activity in the Spirit. In effect, Paul is counseling the Thessalonians to keep exploring the ever increasing life of the Spirit. The Spirit which generates the community should not be stifled. Paul does not curb the growth and enthusiasm of the Thessalonians; rather, he urges that they keep going in a mature, responsible fashion.

At the heart of these brief, staccato words of advice is the vision that the power of God is at work in the midst of the community's life. Verse 18 is more than a truism. To say that God's will in Christ Jesus for the Thessalonians is to "give thanks in every situation" means that the community can actually respond to every moment as coming from the divine patron. A thankful response means that the benefit cycle can continue to build ever further increases of divine grace for the community. Another example is the advice "not to regard prophecy as nothing" (v. 20). This means that the instructions on how to continue to build the community and encourage one another come from within (see 1 Cor. 14:3). Finally, the letter must be seen within a liturgical context (1:2-10; 5:27). As such, the letter becomes a commentary on the very liturgical activity of the Thessalonians, thereby opening up the possibility that what is going on within their gatherings has transcendent implications.

This letter has definite advice for our time. It challenges church leaders and laity as to the way in which they proclaim the Gospel. Leaders who recommend, give advice, rebuke, and so forth, must ask if they have put their words on the line through personal involvement. Also, do the laity leave the proclamation to an elite? Moreover, is the power of the gospel actually denied by those who would prepackage the gospel in slick and macho presentations? Does the gospel enter into the weakness and dark sides of our lives? Furthermore, this letter represents a challenge to those who maintain that a "grass roots" approach to the gospel needs institutional guarantees. Does not the claim that such spontaneous efforts die out without structure conflict with the claim of this letter?

GOSPEL: JOHN 1:6-8, 19-28

Today's Gospel seems very much a variation on last week's theme. One can quite easily detect how certain underlying questions continued to haunt the early Jesus communities. We have already alluded last week to the competitive relationship between the followers of John and those of Jesus. Evidently both sides were making claims of Messiahship for their respective leaders for some time after their deaths. That Jesus may have been involved originally in John's movement could well have fueled the debate. We have also seen in last week's Gospel how thoroughly Mark subordinated John to Jesus. Even more so is it true for today's passage.

The selection for today actually comes from two different parts of chapter 1. Verses 6-8 are part of the introduction to the entire Gospel. Many scholars view these verses as an intrusion into what appears to be a pre-Johannine hymn. Another suggestion is that they are part of a midrashic commentary, which has been converted into an introduction. In either case, these verses function specifically to clear up any question as to the relation between the Baptizer and Jesus. What follows in vv. 19-28 is a further instance of this subordination of John to Jesus.

It should also be underlined that this material can lose much by being too familiar. What sense would a reader have of these verses, particularly vv. 19-28, without certain presuppositions? How comprehensible are vv. 19-21 without some prior knowledge? Where do the titles of "Anointed," "Elijah," and "Prophet" come from? Are we not already in some long-standing conversation? Do we not have to go back to traditional echoes and historical nuances to tease out the meaning? Furthermore, the Johannine piece goes beyond the Markan narrative. We should first note the dramatic construction in vv. 19-28. Here we have a dialogue between John and representatives of "the Judeans." Opposition is provided in the form of inquiring priests and Levites (v. 19) and those sent by the Pharisees (v. 24). The Baptizer makes it clear to them that he is not any of the expected eschatological figures (the "prophet" refers to the one promised by Moses; see Deut. 18:15). Then he indicates what his subordinate role is (vv. 26-27). As is the case with other Johannine dialogues we can see how this interchange progresses, leading deeper and deeper to the question of Jesus' identity (vv. 29-34 introduce the positive testimony of John regarding the identity of Jesus).

But why is this later Gospel still concerned with the question of the relationship between John and Jesus? First, we pointed out last week that followers of the Baptizer existed for over three hundred years and represented a competitive threat in certain areas. It is also probable that some of the original members of the Johannine community came from the Baptizer's movement (vv. 35-39 support this). Thus, such verses would intimate the earliest layer of the Johannine community's development. There is a third issue here. This scene reflects the later Johannine situation where this sect, now divorced from the synagogue, needed to establish clear lines of social identity (hence, the pejorative term "the Judeans"). In other words, this dramatic delineation of Jesus' identity emerges from the group's concern for social definition. The focal point of their identity is located in the figure of Jesus. The function of the Baptizer is to make perfectly clear not only his role but where the community now stands.

Such a concern for social definition is ours today. Certainly we see ourselves as individuals first of all. But there is still need to recognize our social reality. It is human to want to belong, but it is crucial to ask: to whom or to what? Does our relationship to Jesus inform our social reality? What are the implications of identifying with the Risen One? Are we willing to accept the social consequences of our trust? We often say or hear that the Risen One calls us to be a people. Are we aware that this entails more than a liturgical response? Have the costs of this identity sunk into our day-to-day dealings with one another? Are we willing to stand out and bear witness to our "discovered" identity?

One should also point out the experiential direction of this material. In other words, as we read this text, we become involved in a conversation that is loaded with mythic meaning. The burden of vv. 19-28 is to make clear through negation where the lines of meaning exist. Verses 29-34 deliver a positive demonstration. But both sections push the listener to experience what is gestured at. This is taken up quite sensitively in vv. 35-51. The early disciples' interaction with the Johannine Jesus is fundamentally experiential. They are invited (as is the listener) to "come and see," that is, to gain insight found only at the level of profound trust. Such a narrative strategy should provide a caution to both preachers and readers who would merely repeat the pattern but miss the experience. This point ties in with John 3:3. To be born "from above" [with the pun on "again"] means to enter into the experience of transcendence. Those who claim one needs to be "born again" are correct to an extent. One needs to experience transcendent life. This is the mark of all the world's mystic traditions. The difficulty is to distinguish the time-bound patterns and formulae from the actual experience. Our communities of faith yearn for such experience. Yet there are very few mystagogues who can enable these communities on their trek to transcendence. And, without this experience of transcendence, there will be no courageous utterance that the mystery of our lives is in our midst.

Fourth Sunday in Advent

Lectionary	First Lesson	Psalm	Second Lesson	Gospel
Revised Common	2 Sam. 7:1-11, 16	Ps. 89:1-4, 19-26 or Luke 1:47-55	Rom. 16:25-27	Luke 1:26-38
Episcopal (BCP)	2 Sam. 7:4, 8-16	Ps. 132:8-15	Rom. 16:25-27	Luke 1:26-38
Roman Catholic	2 Sam. 7:1-5, 8b-12, 14a, 16	Ps. 89:2-5, 27, 29	Rom. 16:25-27	Luke 1:26-38
Lutheran (LBW)	2 Sam. 7:(1-7)8-11, 16	Ps. 89:1-4, 14-18	Rom. 16:25-27	Luke 1:26-38

FIRST LESSON: 2 SAMUEL 7:1-16

The first lesson from 2 Samuel is, at least, a twice-told tale. The seventh chapter of 2 Samuel is a composite piece, a sixth-century revision of what might well be a tenth-century oracle concerning the Davidic dynasty. The original material (vv. 2-7, 11b, 16) presents the promise of an unending Davidic dynasty. Where David is desirous of building a permanent shrine ("house," v. 5b), the Lord responds surprisingly through the prophet Nathan that, instead, the Lord will build a dynasty ("house," v. 11b) for David. This material, suggesting the prosperity of David's line, would have been a fitting preface to the Succession Document (2 Samuel 9–20; 1 Kings 1–2), composed during the early years of Solomon's reign and used as a source for the later Deuteronomistic revision.

The Deuteronomistic layer decidedly changes the tone and direction of the earlier material. Verse 1 provides the setting for the following story. Although vv. 12, 14-15 continue to speak of a dynastic future, the vision of an unending dynasty is now refocused upon the immediate successor, Solomon. Furthermore, the promise is made contingent upon Solomon's good behavior (v. 14). Verse 13 is added to make the "house" prophecy consistent with Solomon's construction of the Temple. Verses 8-9 amplify the earlier oracle, while vv. 10-11a tend to emphasize national interests (which would speak very much to an exiled people).

From the perspective of the later revision the monarchy becomes part of the deepened ethical reflection of Israel. The promise of a successful monarchy is no longer enough for the people of Israel. A genuine king is one who maintains a faithful relationship with the God of Israel. Further-more, this vision of a faithful king can become the basis for the renewal of Israel's relationship with Yahweh (cf. Ps. 89:1-4, 19-52).

For us today there is much to learn from our ancestors in faith. At the very heart of the earliest layer is the surprising response by Yahweh. The

God of Israel is not a domesticated divinity. This is a sovereign God who prefers to break out with hope rather than to be hemmed in. Moreover, chastened by their national devastation and exile, the people of Israel learned that fidelity is the basis of lasting governance. Leaders without such a sense of responsibility may soon be startled out of their game plans by the unanticipated signals of a living God.

What also should not be lost on the modern reader is the fact that the underlying dreams of such a legitimate monarchy continued to haunt and drive the people of Israel. The two Jewish Wars of Independence (66–73 C.E., 132–135 C.E.) illustrate how some bravely kept this dream alive. Certainly, in our Gospel reading for today we find another attempt to connect with this unfulfilled hope (Luke 1:32-33). We may even understand the subsequent disputes among the "peoples of the Book" as dynastic struggles, arising from disparate (and sometimes tragic) interpretations of such ancient material.

SECOND LESSON: ROMANS 16:25-27

The second reading for today has been the subject of much scholarly debate in regard to its origin and position in Romans. The problematic situation of these verses is compounded by the question whether Romans 16 was originally part of Paul's epistle to Rome. Although Rom. 15:33 seems to end the letter with a concluding offer of peace, Rom. 16:1ff. surprisingly adds a recommendation for Phoebe and an extended list of personal greetings. Now it is unlikely that Paul personally knew such a large number of Christians in Rome. The list, moreover, contains several names that really belong to Asia Minor (Prisca and Aquila, Epainetus, Andronicus). The best solution of these problems is that chapter 16 was not originally directed to Rome, but was a letter of recommendation and greeting originally sent to Ephesus which was attached to the letter of Romans at a later date.

The manuscript evidence for today's second reading increases the bewilderment. There is textual evidence for at least six different locations of these three verses. While most manuscripts place this material at the end of Romans 16 (that is, after 16:23 or 16:24), a number of other manuscripts put the doxology after Rom. 14:23; still another places it after Rom. 15:33. Additionally, the vocabulary and ideas strongly suggest non-Pauline authorship. Because of its questionable textual history and its rather un-Pauline character, Rom. 16:25-27 would seem to be a later interpolation into the text. The passage gives us a vivid example of how unsettled were the manuscripts of the first two centuries.

It seems clear, however, that whatever the position of these verses, they were written with a view to an entire letter to the Romans, not just for chapter 16. In other words, Rom. 16:25-27 might be a trace of the second-century revision of Pauline material. Indeed, the phrase "prophetic writings" (v. 26) could reflect a second-century collection (2 Pet. 3:16). Some scholars have wondered whether this material is actually a Marcionite conclusion, while others see an anti-Marcionite ending. Although this debate cannot be decided, it is apparent that epistles from those who consider themselves in the Pauline tradition (such as Ephesians, Colossians, and 1 Tim. 3:16) share the same vocabulary and ideological assumptions.

The verses themselves form an extended doxology. There is the designation of the one praised ("to the one who," "to the only wise God"), the praise uttered ("be glory"), the indication of time ("for ever"), and the confirmatory "Amen." As a doxology it might well mirror the liturgical language of the time. But this is no simple doxology. The entire piece is well crafted. Three prepositional phrases ("according to my gospel, . . . the preaching of Jesus Christ, . . . the revelation of the mystery") depend on an introductory infinitive while the central idea is defined by three participial statements ("kept secret, . . . disclosed, . . . made known") before the final solemnity in v. 27a discloses to whom the doxology is ascribed.

The doxology is written from a second-century understanding of Paul the apostle. Instead of an end time soon to come, there is the "revelation long kept secret now manifest." The eschatological emphasis is replaced by a cosmic present. While there is still a mission "to all the Gentiles," there is no corresponding urgency before the end arrives. Further, the Hellenistic notion of prophetic writings as revelatory seems to undergird v. 26b (especially if the "writings" include Pauline material). It would thus appear that the doxology functions to express not simply an overview of the Pauline career but more a basis for maintaining Paul's vision for a later generation. This prayer of thanksgiving is simultaneously one of hope that the new audience become "strengthened" according to the traditions which reveal what is truly at stake.

But what do these critical remarks have to do with congregations of today? It is important to see even in this fragment the development of the early Jesus movement. Indeed, these verses ask us whether we still experience our traditions as revelatory. Does our reading of Scripture enable us to understand that God is mysteriously present in our midst? Do we believe that Wisdom is within our experience? Are we able to recognize the One who would disclose to us what we continually fail to notice? Can we continue to build creatively our traditions and allow them to become access points to God?

GOSPEL: LUKE 1:26-38

In touching on today's Gospel we shall focus our commentary upon the imaginative breakthrough of this text. There is a tendency to regard scenes of the Gospel tradition as monuments rather than to appreciate the underlying movement that reaches out beyond the well-known confines of the story. Especially in regard to the scene of Annunciation we need to be careful not to condemn our reading to a simple repetition or to a fixated interpretation. Here the history of art can be instructive. Each generation of artist attempts a new interpretation of what appears at first blush a stylized scene. We need to be cautious of our own theological and cultural agenda which would foreclose the possibility that this passage actually has something new to say to us.

Two historical points should be kept in mind. First, Luke evidently has drawn upon the messianic hopes of the Jewish people (as well as on the format for such an angelic appearance). Second, the claim of divine origin has definite political ramifications. In the ancient world historical leaders who figured in the "salvation" of civilization would usually be credited with divine origin. In other words, the import of such an origin was both theological and social. Luke has taken such patterns of hope and security and has applied them to what the Greco-Roman world would consider a most unlikely candidate.

Luke, however, goes beyond a mere duplication of traditional forms. There is more here than propaganda or messianic speculation. In vv. 35ff. we come to a most distinctive note. Gabriel's response to Mary's objection gives us a profound insight into the question of Jesus' relation to God. Mary asks the question that gets to the radical nature of who Jesus is for Christians. In so doing she goes to the limit of human hope and asks if God has something to say. The heavenly messenger declares that this child is totally the work of God, that God has gone beyond the demands and expectations of humanity by surprising us with a new creation. In pushing back the christological speculation concerning the conferral of divine sonship upon Jesus from the moment of resurrection (Rom. 1:4), or of enthronement (Heb. 1:3), or of even baptism (Mark 1:11), to the moment of conception, the writer attempts to outdistance imaginatively the surprising births of the heroes of Israel and the Hellenistic world.

There is perhaps an even more surprising note. As many commentators and preachers have pointed out, everything hangs upon the final utterance of Mary. While many have used this verse to bolster patriarchal power relationships, what we find here is the entrance of the human into the divine project. Indeed, divinity stands helpless without Mary's consent. While nothing is impossible with God, it would have been impossible without

Mary. One is almost overwhelmed by the reverence the angelic figure has for this declaration of human freedom.

It is crucial for both preacher and congregation to appreciate the startling elements of this passage. It should not be a question of proof-texting later dogmatic assertions as it is a matter of coming to grips with the claim that something new of God has come to us and that we are invited to enter freely into this unfinished story. What would happen if our churches began to take seriously the personal, social, and political ramifications of such a vision? What would happen if we really began to imagine that the power of the Most High overshadows us? How long could we hold on to our neuroses, power games, and social injustices? What would happen if we acted on the nonviolent beckoning of God?

Finally, a note on angels. Some modern readers will immediately balk at the note of such an implausible scene. Others will more "scientifically" reduce the scene to an imaginary projection at best. In both instances, the reader uncritically applies one's own modern assumptions upon the ancient story. It would be better to ask what such a manifestation meant in the ancient world before imposing one's categories. The ancients believed that communication was possible between the divine and human realms. An angelic apparition meant precisely this breakthrough in communication. If a modern reader is to understand the text, then one needs to consider the various ways in which communication breakthroughs occur in one's existence. This is where "angels" occur today. Do we ever have a sense that there is more intimated in our experience than what is given in the ordinary ways of speech? Do we, now and again, tiptoe on the edge of mystery—even at the bedsides of our children or aged parents? What would happen if we allowed the terror and mystery of those moments to sink in on us? Would we hear the angels sing?

The Nativity of Our Lord I
Christmas Eve

Lectionary	First Lesson	Psalm	Second Lesson	Gospel
Revised Common	Isa. 9:2-7	Psalm 96	Titus 2:11-14	Luke 2:1-14 (15-20)
Episcopal (BCP)	Isa. 9:2-4, 6-7	Psalm 96	Titus 2:11-14	Luke 2:1-14 (15-20)
Roman Catholic	Isa. 9:2-7	Ps. 96:1-3, 11-13	Titus 2:11-14	Luke 2:1-14
Lutheran (LBW)	Isa. 9:2-7	Psalm 96	Titus 2:11-14	Luke 2:1-20

FIRST LESSON: ISAIAH 9:2-7

Our first lesson for today comes originally out of a time of political intrigue and historical upheaval. If Isa. 9:1, functioning as a transition from the teaching of Isaiah the prophet (8:11-22) to the messianic hymn of Isa. 9:2-7, can be used to date the material, then it would have been delivered after the annexation in 733 B.C.E. of the land of Zebulun, Naphtali, and Galilee by Assyria (cf. 2 Kings 15:29). By reading carefully through the highly edited material (5:8—10:4), one can get a dramatic impression of the terror of an unsettled political atmosphere. Hope and fear were encountered at every border. Ahaz, the king of Judah, had been unnerved by the threatening developments of the Syro-Ephraimite war (734–733 B.C.E.). To counter the Northern Kingdom's political alliances, he sought alignment with the major political force, Assyria (2 Kings 16), despite the warning of Isaiah the prophet (Isa. 7:4, 16-17; 8:4-8a).

The reading for today is actually the end piece of what has been called traditionally the "testimony of Isaiah" (6:1—9:7). This collection of material has been sandwiched between two other clusters of oracles (oracles of doom against the leaders in Judah and Ephraim, the Northern Kingdom). All of this material can be dated to the period surrounding the Syro-Ephraimite conflict. It is rather surprising to find within the centerpiece of this edited grouping such a positive passage. Indeed, coming directly after the threatening remarks of Isaiah 8 and preceding the woeful lesson of Ephraim's fall for Judah (9:8—10:4), Isa. 9:2-7 presents a startling reversal of the historical predicament of Judah.

In focusing upon the passage for today, one can detect not only an evident editorial hand in Isa. 9:1 but also in v. 2 a note of "darkness into light" picking up the "darkness" and "gloom" of 8:22. Second, the birth of a child as a prophetic sign is consistent with other parts of the first book of Isaiah (e.g., 7:14; 8:3). Scholars have pointed out that vv. 2-7 may well have been modeled upon the hymns celebrating the enthronement of a king. Indeed, the extraordinary terms of praise (v. 6cd) are commonplace items in ancient Near Eastern eulogies for monarchs. However, there is a decided difference in this material. Instead of looking to the past, or even to a present celebration, the hymn looks to a future Davidic monarch, whose dynasty will have no end. This utopian rule will be characterized by justice (v. 7) for a peaceful (v. 5), free (v. 4), and flourishing (v. 3) people. Thus, in the very midst of political uncertainty a word of hope comes forth from the prophet. Later on, Cyrus, who brought an end to the Babylonian exile, would be viewed along these lines (Isaiah 44–45). Yet, as the subsequent history of interpretation by both Jews and Christians indicates, these verses remained extremely fecund.

For the modern interpreter there is the almost irresistible temptation to link this passage immediately to the Christmas story. Of course, there is much tradition in favor of such an interpretive move. But, it might be advisable for the preacher to return to the historical issues of the Isaianic material. As suggested above, this passage—in its own time—attempted to go beyond the political quagmire of eighth-century Judah. This utopian vision was based upon the insight that the political position of Judah always rested upon the reality of its theological orientation. In other words, for Isaiah, there was no merely political problem or solution. Rather, in the very practical affairs of state and national security the theological question must be raised. If we permit the challenge of this passage to touch our time, we also must ask whether our political agenda allow for such theological scrutiny. Do our political decisions reflect a vision of faith, or do we actually behave as if we were in total control? Can we even imagine a God who does not play by our game plans? The early Jesus believers did and caught the surprising signal from their ancestor in faith. Can we?

SECOND LESSON: TITUS 2:11-14

The second lesson for today comes from one of three pseudonymous letters written sometime between 100 and 140 C.E. Traditionally known as the Pastoral Letters, 1 and 2 Timothy and Titus reflect the organizational, cultural, and theological concerns of the church in Asia Minor that has gone beyond the grass roots communities of the earlier Pauline era.

Most New Testament scholars point out that the language (in both style and content) of the Pastorals differs significantly from the accepted Pauline letters. Furthermore, the inserted liturgical elements, the lengthy regulations regarding the selection and appointment of church officers, and the repetitive ethical lists of virtues and vices, suggest a later situation. What is usually overlooked, however, is that the Pastorals were but one version of the Pauline tradition in the second century. There were other serious interpreters claiming Pauline heritage. Gnostics, Marcionites, and Montanists, in their own ways, considered themselves to be the authentic carriers of Paul's vision. Even the *Acts of Paul and Thecla* point to a more charismatic, countercultural experiment of the Pauline tradition. Thus, the Pastorals' pseudonymity was deliberately chosen in order to convince listeners that the author's understanding of Paul was the correct version.

As we see throughout the Letter to Titus (the itinerant preacher turned resident official), the Pastoral version of the Pauline tradition entailed a particular understanding of church, its social life and leadership. Charismatic authority was severely curtailed (1:10-16), while institutional officers were sanctioned (1:5-9). The task of the genuine leader was to settle disputes, maintain order, and provide a model for social respectability. The social code that the anonymous writer counsels (2:1-10) consciously supports the social virtues of the Roman Empire (including the institution of slavery, 2:9-10). The writer desires that no one should "look down" on these Christians (2:15), for they ought to outstrip all in the very deeds which keep the empire a going concern.

According to Titus, what distinguishes Christians from other peoples of the empire is not their behavior but the fundamental motivation for their actions. In our reading for today the writer presents the visionary basis for behavior. It is telling that the traditional message is clothed in the language of the imperial culture. There is nothing in the language, for example, in vv. 11-12 that is distinctively Christian. The theology of the empire already broadcast the propaganda that the divine (acting through the emperors) brings benefits (grace) to all. The avoidance of impiety and the control of passions (v. 12) were behavioral goals of all those who had been "educated" for a civil life. Even words describing the "manifestation" or "epiphany" of the "glory" of the "great God and Savior" are part of the imperial language game. The difference is quite specific. It is no longer the imperial cult that provides the benefits and security for life. Instead, the "philanthropy" of God the Savior (3:4) has "appeared" (cf. 2:11). The Pauline notion of undeserved grace continues here (3:5) as the new hero Jesus Christ performs the ultimate act of sacrifice in order to gain a special people (2:14). Moreover, the eschatological hope of Paul is still preserved (2:13) as the writer advises his audience to "wait for the blessed hope and manifestation." At the same time, the writer describes the people as "zealous for good deeds [works]" (2:14). This is hardly a Pauline direction. In short, in order to sustain his interpretation of the Pauline tradition, the writer of Titus embeds the Christian message within the language of the imperial culture.

The writer of Titus creatively faced what preachers today must constantly consider: how to transmit the Christian tradition into new times and situations. A simple repetition of Titus' solution will not do. Indeed, there are many who think that Titus' response was severely limited. Rather, we must ask ourselves what is our vision of God's presence to us. What words and images express the mystery at the core of our lives? For without this labor of translation we shall not sustain one another in the coming years.

GOSPEL: LUKE 2:1-20

(For Luke 2:15-20 see the Gospel for the feast of the Name of Jesus [January 1], below.)

The familiar Lukan Christmas story has been rendered practically innocuous in Western culture. We read it nostalgically from a private perspective. Rarely does anyone see the larger political threat of this material.

We can begin to get a glimpse of the Lukan vision by pedantically noticing that the first section is fraught (vv. 1-5) with historical problems. Basically, the point is that Luke has not presented an accurate historical account. The existence of such a worldwide census, the linkage of Quirinius (6 C.E.) with the time of Herod (4 B.C.E.), the very manner of Joseph's return to his ancestral town—all are quite problematic. Attempts to resolve these difficulties fail. We must reckon with either Luke's mistakes or his revision of events for his own theological purpose. Moving along the lines of the latter alternative, we can see that Luke has provided his story with a most solemn introduction, linking the birth of Jesus to the powers of this world. Not only does Luke make the traditional connections with the figure and promise of David the King, he also sets the birth of Jesus over against the emperor, whose birthday had been understood as that of "the god who has marked the beginning of the good news for the world" (Priene Inscription). The census functions as the means of the Spirit to bring about the divine plan of salvation.

The second part (vv. 6-7) is more concerned with noting that Jesus is born in a feeding trough than with the birth itself or with the question of the family's lodging. There may well be an influence of Isa. 1:3 (LXX), where a reversal of the Isaian picture is produced. Further, the "wrapping" of Jesus indicates, not poverty, but careful attention. Jesus is thus born in the town of David, in a feeding trough where God sustains the people.

The main focus of the passage, however, is found in the next section (vv. 8-14). The appearance of the heavenly messenger to the shepherds provides an occasion to show clearly who Jesus is. The format of this section is basically that of an angelic annunciation (the appearance of divine

presence evokes a fearful response, a command to fear not, a declaration of
meaning, and, finally, a sign that will be confirmed). It is quite significant
that the appearance is made to shepherds. For the Jews, shepherds were
considered as outside the law. Thus we have an instance of God's breakthrough to the alienated.

But there is another possible way of understanding the text. The Roman
world hungered for peace. Virgil, in his Fourth Eclogue, delivered a vision
of the world once again at peace, a golden age that regained the pastoral
simplicity of human life. It could well be that Luke, in light of vv. 1-3, is
reiterating the Christian counterclaim that the age of peace has come, not
through Augustus, but through the advent of Jesus. Indeed, the canticle of
the heavenly army is a statement both theological and political. In a new
way this canticle repeats the basic Christian witness: that God has definite-
ly acted in Jesus and that this action has changed the very course of events.

This last point forms the basis for reflection on the entire text. We are
called to see in this infancy narrative an impossible vision—that God has
set us on the path of global peace. This vision does not lead us backward in
time or place but calls us to consider the consequences of this vision for our
human future on this planet.

The Nativity of Our Lord 2
Christmas Day

Lectionary	First Lesson	Psalm	Second Lesson	Gospel
Revised Common	Isa. 52:7-10	Psalm 98	Heb. 1:1-4 (5-12)	John 1:1-14
Episcopal (BCP)	Isa. 52:7-10	Psalm 98	Heb. 1:1-12	John 1:1-14
Roman Catholic	Isa. 52:7-10	Ps. 98:1-6	Heb. 1:1-6	John 1:1-18
Lutheran (LBW)	Isa. 52:7-10	Psalm 98	Heb. 1:1-9	John 1:1-14

FIRST LESSON: ISAIAH 52:7-10

The first lesson today comes from Second Isaiah. (For comments on the general background of Second Isaiah, see above on the first lesson for the Second Sunday of Advent.) Once again the prophet envisions the unimaginable for an exiled people: a return to their homeland instead of historical extinction. Moreover, today's passage gives another example of the creativity of the prophet in proclaiming his novel message.

Isaiah 52:7-10 is part of a larger complex of material (51:9—52:12). This complex begins with a song set in lament format (51:9-16). After a typical appeal made to the Divine Warrior to rouse from sleep and come to the aid of his clients, the Lord responds, suggesting that those who appeal have forgotten the very nature of their God. Nevertheless, the oppressed shall be free (v. 14). The next section appears, at first blush, to be another lament. In fact, although it begins with a call to awake, it is not made to the Lord. Instead, this is actually a call for Jerusalem to get up. The devastating time is over, as the Lord removes their "cup of staggering" and gives it to their tormentors (v. 23). A lament has been turned into a prophetic oracle (vv. 21-23). A third wake-up call comes in 52:1. Once again, it is Jerusalem who is summoned to put on festal garments and rise up from the dust of defeat. Here there is no question of lament; rather, it is a call to celebration. The reading for today probably followed 52:1-2 originally; the intervening section (52:3-6) is a later insertion. Verses 11-12 touch on the exodus from Babylon. The people are to return purified, in good order, and secure in the protection of the Lord.

The focus changes strikingly through this complex of material. The appeal to Yahweh becomes a call for Jerusalem to wake up and hear the astounding news. What one finds in 52:7-10 is a marvelous sound and sight piece. The arrival of the "good news" is dramatically presented. First, an allusion to the messenger's running upon the mountains; then, the beating of feet is replaced by the messenger's announcement: "Your God reigns!" The sound wave continues in v. 8a as Jerusalem is told to "listen," and the city's "sentinels lift up their voices" in song. They break out in song for they now see "the return of the LORD to Zion," that is, the first caravans of returnees. The "ruins of Jerusalem" are commanded to sing out at the comforting of the people. Indeed, this scene is envisioned "before the eyes of all the nations" (v. 10).

The boldness of this material becomes evident when one recalls that this material originated some time before the exiles were sent home by Cyrus. This material, especially 52:7-10, is a rehearsal of the future. The call to awake is directed, first of all, to those in exile to begin to reimagine their lives out of such an astonishing hope. Such hope was founded upon a discovery of who God is. To sing out "God reigns" was not a war cry of the oppressor but a startled response by people who find the compassion of God in the midst of their despair. Can the echoes of this ancient song still find a home in the modern heart? Are we willing to wake up and hear the surprising presence of God?

SECOND LESSON: HEBREWS 1:1-12

Perhaps the most unfortunate response to today's second lesson would be indifference. It is quite likely that the modern audience, on one hand, would simply expect such language to be applied to the figure of Jesus, or, on the other, would find little relevance in such outmoded speech. Few would be upset by the radical claim laid at the outset of and maintained throughout the extended homily known as the Letter to the Hebrews.

This so-called letter from the outset has been shrouded in mystery. Both ancient and modern commentators are unsure of its author, except to conclude that it was not Paul. The addressees are traditionally termed "Hebrews" simply due to the "Jewish" content in the treatise. Yet other volumes of the New Testament use typical Jewish motifs and scriptural references for Gentile audiences (e.g., Galatians). Although reference to the Temple is made as if in the present, the writer was not interested in the actual Herodian Temple. Rather, he wished to depict the cult of the desert as found in Hebrew Scripture. While Hebrews has traditionally been dated to about 95–96 C.E. (due to its use by 1 Clement), it could have been written as late as 110 C.E. Finally, even the argument surrounding the figure of Jesus is not historical as much as it is exegetical, employing Scripture in a most creative fashion.

There is, then, little left but the words. Yet from the text alone one can detect that the original audience had been Christian for some time (5:12), had experienced persecution in the past (10:32-34) and could expect more in the future (12:3-13; 13:3). The task for the writer of Hebrews was to inspire a distant community to endure what might have been a crisis of confidence. This was done through a consummate work of persuasion, providing a christological basis for the community's faithful response.

Today's lesson, the opening to the entire homily, is a magnificent illustration of this rhetorical mastery at the service of the community. Hebrews 1:1-12 is actually part of the first major section of Hebrews. (1:1—2:18). The passage at hand can be divided into two portions. The first four verses (actually one long periodic sentence) form the *exordium* (rhetorical opening) to the entire work. Verses 5-12 are a well-crafted set of scriptural citations, which build upon the key images disclosed in the beginning rhetorical salvo.

In vv. 1-4 it is important to hear the "pomp and circumstances" of the piece. The rhetorical complexity of the material reflects the importance of the occasion. Verses 1-2 introduce the foundation and source of theological reflection for Hebrews, namely, God's speaking. This has occurred in times past and now happens through a "Son." With the mention of "Son," come traditional themes of creation, wisdom, and enthronement. The writer paints an awesome picture of this heroic figure, bearing the mythic mantle of creation and the glory of God, and being enthroned as the rightful inheritor of the cosmos. Immediately there is a flourish of scriptural citations (v. 5—Ps. 2:7; 2 Sam. 7:14; v. 6—Deut. 32:43 (LXX); v. 7—Ps. 104:4; vv. 8-9—Ps. 45:6-7; vv. 10-12—Ps. 102:25-27; v. 13—Ps. 110:1), which construct an impressive sight.

What should not be lost on the modern reader is how odd this application would be for the figure of Jesus. Such awesome speech was associated with the elite at the top of the ancient social pyramid (including angels), not with a nobody. Yet, this crucial connection is at the heart of this work. For the very humanity of Jesus proves to be the access point to the divine. No one in the ancient world would miss the radical overturning of the social order through this enthronement scene. Jesus has journeyed into God, made an exodus into the divine realm for others to follow. There is a future for humanity because there has been that "one small step" of a man. Even creation itself takes on a human face.

GOSPEL: JOHN 1:1-18

In contrast to the more traditional Christmas narratives, today's Gospel inaugurates this season of joy on a level unparalleled in the Gospel tradition. Some scholars find, in what has been fittingly called the overture to the Gospel of John, elements of a hymn that may have had its origin as a pre-Christian poem about a heavenly revealer of God.

Yet great disagreement exists as to the specific verses of the hymn. Certainly vv. 6-8 and 15 are polemical interpolations that subordinate the Baptizer to the Word made flesh. Although v. 9 can be associated with v. 5, it seems to fit in well with this polemic. Verses 12c and 13 provide an explanation of the hymnic verses, 12a and b, about how human beings become God's children. Verse 16 is probably a secondary addition to the hymn itself, while vv. 17 and 18 explain "love following love." Thus, at least, vv. 1-5, 10-12b, 14 form what many scholars would describe as a hymn. Indeed, one can see a wonderful step-by-step connection. For example, vv. 1-2 can be denoted: beginning → Word → Word → God → God → Word → (Word) → beginning → God).

What should not be lost in this analysis is the majestic movement of the prologue, which takes off from the assertion of the divine origin of the Word to a witness of the Christian community's faith in the Word embodied in Jesus. At the same time, we should recognize the creativity of the Johannine community, which may well have taken a heavenly wisdom hymn (see Sirach 24) in order to plumb the mystery of the One who has risen and lives in their midst. In the Wisdom writings there is the tradition not only that Wisdom was present at the creation but also that Lady Wisdom dwelt among humans (Proverbs 8; Wis. Sol. 7:27).

While vv. 1 and 2, 3-5, 10-12b can be reconciled with traditional notions about wisdom, v. 14 presents a radical break with both Jewish and Hellenistic speculation. Here is sung the paradox that the eternally preexistent divine Word has entered into limited human existence. The community, moreover, asserts that this divine presence is capable of being humanly experienced (vv. 14c, 16). In fact, it becomes the genuine source of human life. Such a claim should not be lost on the modern Bible reader. The ancient imagination could not conceive of the possibility of the divine entering fully into human experience. Especially when death came, the gods were far off. It was acceptable to the divine to appear to be human, but that was as far as it would go. For the divine to "pitch its tent" and take up residence beggared the first-century mind. It is probably as unsettling to the modern.

Recently, another structural option has been suggested, namely, that what we have is not a hymn but a sustained Christian interpretation of Gen. 1:1-5. John 1:1-5 would form a primary exposition, while vv. 6-18 would deliver further elaboration. In effect, we would have a Jewish paraphrase suggesting that the creation is presently happening, that the words of Genesis have come into their own. This second interpretation avoids the wrangling over the hymnic structure and locates this revision in a Jewish-Christian context.

Furthermore, there are two major textual difficulties for the translator. The troublesome v. 4 should be rendered more literally: "That which had come to be in him was life." Creation is not what is emphasized here; rather it is the function of the Word. Second, in v. 18, the better manuscripts read, "the only God," not "God the only Son." The high Christology of John, as well as the principle of the more difficult reading, supports this profound direction.

From its beginning, the passage is replete with scriptural references—for example, Genesis 1 and Exod. 25:8 and 9. Significant themes and motifs are found later in the Gospel. Verse 11 sums up chaps. 1–12; v. 12, chaps. 13–20. While such interesting connections can be made, what stands out most emphatically is the poetry of the piece itself. What speaks to us in these familiar and human terms is the very heart of God.

First Sunday after Christmas

Lectionary	First Lesson	Psalm	Second Lesson	Gospel
Revised Common	Isa. 61:10—62:3	Psalm 148	Gal. 4:4-7	Luke 2:22-40
Episcopal (BCP)	Isa. 61:10—62:3	Psalm 147	Gal. 3:23-25; 4:4-7	John 1:1-18
Roman Catholic	Gen. 15:1-6; 21:1-3	Psalm 128	Heb. 11:8, 11-12, 17-19	Luke 2:22-40
Lutheran (LBW)	Isa. 45:22-25	Psalm 111	Col. 3:12-17	Luke 2:25-40

FIRST LESSON: ISAIAH 45:22-25; 61:10—62:3; GENESIS 15:1-6; 21:1-3

ISAIAH 45:22-25

Today's selection from Isaiah 45 represents the hard-won insight of an exiled people. Verses 22-25 are part of a larger speech (Isa. 45:11-25) which magnificently counters the political and theological assumptions of the neo-Babylonian Empire. Instead of celebrating the imperial god Marduk as bestower of order and legitimator of the political status quo, these lines proclaim the God of exiles to be the founder of the world.

Students of religion usually point out that it was during the exilic period that Israel discovered the implications of a genuine and thoroughgoing monotheism. Yet such reflective language does not do full justice to the stunning vision of Second Isaiah. The conviction that the God of Israel is the Creator of the cosmos (v. 23) and ultimate source of justice (v. 24) comes out of the devastating experience of what should have been the extinction of a people. Going to the edge of nothingness brought the profound recognition of God as the creative heart of the universe. This creative activity of God further manifested itself for the poet both in the messianic mission of Cyrus and in the envisioned return of the oppressed people to Jerusalem.

The challenge before the modern reader is quite stark. Do we believe that God is truly the God of all the earth and its peoples (v. 22)? Or, are there places and persons wherein we cannot imagine the presence of God? Is not this reluctance to find the living God throughout the planet a result of our idolatry (Isa. 45:20)? Have we not constructed images of ourselves and others to keep the heart of mystery at bay? When shall we finally hear the invitation to return to the only One?

ISAIAH 61:10—62:3

(For an analysis of Isaiah 61 please see the first lesson for the Third Sunday of Advent [Isa. 61:1-4, 8-11].)

In this selection from Third Isaiah (for background on Third Isaiah, see the first lesson for the First Sunday of Advent) we hear the poetic strains echoing once more amid the ruins of Jerusalem. As noted earlier, Isa. 61:10-11 functions as a song of thanksgiving (and the conclusion to 61:1-11), where the poet identifies himself with the future glory of Jerusalem. Decked out in both priestly and wedding metaphors, these verses confidently anticipate the rebuilding of the people's lives and land. Isaiah 62:1-3, the second part of today's reading, is actually the opening section of an extended piece (62:1-12). In v. 1 the poet declares his ardent prayer for the utopian promise of Jerusalem. His persistent wish is continued in v. 2. Most significant for this poetic piece is the promise of a new name to be bestowed by Yahweh. As is well known, the giving of a new name in the biblical tradition indicates a change in direction or future (cf. Gen. 17:5-15; 32:28). Here the change intimated is a remarkable transformation of a ruined city and people into a glorious and delightful community. Although v. 4 is not part of today's reading, it would be advisable to note the concrete shift in names ("Forsaken" to "My Delight is in Her," "Desolate" to "Married") that dramatically indicate the radical revision of the people's future. The third verse employs the imagery of royal investiture, once more reaffirming the community as a "royal people."

For the modern reader much may be lost in this brief reading. The two poetic segments attempted to summon up an imaginative vision for a people living still among the ruins. The festive and confident tones should not drown out the empty spaces of a devastated city. Indeed, for those living at that time, the hopeful strains would have been the more difficult sounds to hear. Moreover, by splicing together material from two different (yet related) pieces, the editors of today's reading allow us to concentrate on the insistent reiteration of hope. The poet's ardent stance in prayer (likewise, in vv. 6-7 the cities sentries are commanded to keep God mindful of the divine promise) follows his celebratory vision of the transformed condition of his people. Such a vision does not disappear with time. As known from the history of Israel, this vision continued to haunt the people. Indeed, one can fruitfully suggest that this material works precisely insofar as it is "unfinished." Could the enduring task for the modern Bible reader be to ask whether we can accept such a transformative possibility among the devastation and depressions of our own lives and society?

GENESIS 15:1-6; 21:1-3

Although today's selections from Genesis are quite brief, they contain a major theme of the first book of the Hebrew Scriptures. The issue of God's promise (and partial fulfillment) comes immediately into focus. Now throughout the extended Abraham cycle of stories (Genesis 12–25) numerous instances of divine promises are followed by obstacles that seem to make such promises impossible to accomplish. Nevertheless, divine intervention overcomes such obstacles by either dramatic deliverance from crises or a fitting provision of human need.

Our lesson for today already comes from two distinct parts of Genesis. Genesis 15:1-6 can be seen as the first section of the two-part story of the covenant with Abraham (15:1-6, 7-21), while Gen. 21:1-3 is a segment of an introduction (Gen. 21:1-6) to the larger story of the relationship between Isaac and Ishmael (Gen. 21:1-21). This latter story is part of the collection of Elohist stories (20:1-22:24) about Abraham. In bringing these two selections together, there has been an editorial attempt to fit the promise of Genesis 15 with the fulfillment of Genesis 21. While such an editorial decision can be justified from the logic of the narrative itself (and the recognition of the multiple layering of the Abrahamic material), it should not be overlooked that this predictable decision may, in fact, prevent the modern reader from detecting other interpretive possibilities in the text.

The first part of our lesson bears a remarkable resemblance to the prophetic formats elsewhere in the Hebrew Scriptures. In v. 1 we hear the familiar "the word of the LORD came to Abram" (cf. Jer. 1:2; Hos. 1:1). Notice that the "word of the LORD" is noted as coming "in a vision." The vision to Abram literally in the Hebrew "says" the oracle in v. 1b. So sight and sound are combined in this narrative. In v. 1b Yahweh assumes a protective role ("your shield") and promises a "very great reward." This last point introduces Abram's response (v. 2) that is laced with anxiety over the future. The fear that one will die without an heir is continued with Abram's complaint in v. 3. That a slave should be an heir to his house would be a grave dishonor. It should not be forgotten that there is no notion of an afterlife resident in this dialogue. Abram's future is tied up directly with his name being carried forward along family lines. Verse 4 presents Yahweh's oracular response. This is dramatically coupled with v. 5, which delivers both another oracular utterance and vision. The sight of innumerable stars becomes a metaphor of promise. The narrative (v. 6) continues with the remark that Abram "trusted" the Lord and that the Lord considered him "righteous."

When one adds the second portion of today's reading, it would seem that the promise has come true. Yet, that is not exactly the case. Certainly

Gen. 15:4 finds fulfillment in Gen. 21:1-3. But the magnificent vision of v. 5 has hardly come to fruition. If this material is part of the Davidic-Solomonic recasting of the old stories of Abraham, then v. 5 would be pointing in the direction of such royal promise. And yet, the suggestive metaphor of v. 5 eludes any easy historical or interpretive closure. Certainly the early Jesus believers detected an opening here.

Finally, what can be said of v. 6? Here the narrator comments on Abram's response to a major life crisis. His complaint (vv. 2-3) brings him to the very limit of his existence. Looking beyond the present, he sees no future. Here the oracle of God comes doubly upon him (vv. 4, 5). Not only will he have an heir to carry on the family name but there will be innumerable descendants. His response is to "trust" this intimation of the infinite. In so doing, Abram becomes a paradigm for those who would enter into genuine relation with Yahweh ("He reckoned it to him as righteousness").

This text can bring the modern Bible reader to the edge of one's life. What do we do in the limit situations of our lives? Where do we go when we feel that there is no way out? How do we meet those moments when the world closes in on us? Others, in the past and in the present, have scanned the skies and have only felt overwhelmed by such infinity. But how many can make the connection that Abram made? Who can see such infinity as a metaphor for one's future? Is this not what the spiritual life is about—living out of the horizon of hope, without any visible means of support?

SECOND LESSON: GALATIANS 3:23-25; 4:4-7; HEBREWS 11:8, 11-12, 17-19; COLOSSIANS 3:12-17

GALATIANS 3:23-25

In the selections from Galatians (3:23-25; 4:4-7) we find Paul addressing Gentile communities who have already received his message and strongly experienced the outbreak of the Spirit. Evidently, after Paul's departure from Galatia, other Jewish missionaries arrived and built upon the Galatians' transcendent experience, advising them to adopt the customs and conditions of Hellenistic Judaism in order to maintain and enhance their life in the Spirit. Paul's letter attempts to dissuade the communities from what is, in his perspective, a denial of the depths of their faith.

Paul's response is quite dramatic. For Paul it was not a matter of "upgrading" one's religious life by taking on an honored and ancient religious tradition. To have entered into the life of faith, to be "in Christ," meant that a new era had begun. What God had accomplished in Christ added a new chapter to God's dealing with Israel and the world. This new situation totally revised what had come before. The covenantal story took on a decidedly different character. Not interested in founding a new religion, Paul proclaimed that the deepest dreams for all humanity were truly possible. To express this radical perspective he employed the conceptual and mythic categories of the Hellenistic world, including the dialectical relationship between custom and experience.

Now Paul's opponents would have understood that Torah represented the positive embodiment of human hopes and culture. The world of Torah held promise for those who invested themselves in its practice. From Paul's point of view this was a fundamental mistake for those Gentiles who had already experienced transcendence in Christ. The breakthrough had come already and no additional insurance or prior condition was needed to live in the Spirit.

The two passages for today (3:23-25; 4:4-7) succinctly bring out these points. From Paul's perspective the Torah (Law, *nomos*) takes on a decidedly negative character. As noted above, this is due to the new insight brought about "in Christ." Just as one can notice shadows only after a light has been turned on in a room, so also one sees the law differently with the coming of the Christ. Utilizing the Hellenistic association of law and education (e.g., Plato, *Laws* 5.730B, 7.808E–810C), Paul inverts the usually positive connection. The law is now seen as limited, confining, and, indicated by his metaphor of the law, a "pedagogue," that is, an attendant slave who served as a rough and rude disciplinarian for a schoolboy. The rhetorical intent of Gal. 3:23-25 is to declare that this situation is no longer so. With the arrival of the age of faith, there is no need to be in a servile condition. This is positively reinforced by 3:26-29 where Paul reminds the Galatians that they are already mature sons and daughter of God. They have attained their transcendental majority.

GALATIANS 4:4-7

Our second selection from Galatians reinforces Paul's argument. Employing what may be elements of an earlier hymn (4:4), Paul brings the purpose of this action to light. While the original hymn may have looked upon the law (*nomos*) in a positive or neutral fashion, Paul redesigns this hymnic fragment into a universal redemptive declaration: to redeem those under the law's constraints and bring "adoption" to all, including the Galatians. It is crucial to understand why Paul emphasizes the point of adoption. Adoption in the ancient world legally conferred genuine "sonship" upon the person. Translations that attempt to be politically correct by using "children" for "sons" miss the legal point. Paul is talking about the attainment of legal standing as mature adults, who possess all the rights of inheritance. In Gal. 3:23-25 we saw that the Galatians have "come of age." Here we see that they are genuinely related with full rights to the Father. Indeed, Paul works inductively in v. 6 to remind the Galatians that their prior ecstatic experience confirms his mythic description. If this is the case, then they are already fully engaged in the divine life and purpose (v. 7).

Although the letter to the Galatians has been often called the "Magna Carta of Christian Liberty," Paul's insight into the reality of life in the Spirit has often been confined quite often to apologetic straitjackets. The excitement of Paul's message came in his fusion of the universal hope of Israel with the utopian drives of the Hellenistic world. He saw that the dreams of genuine human life could be realized in Christ. The Galatians did not comprehend the implications of their own experience. They already had what they thought they lacked. His letter attempts to bring them back to their own experience and to see the power and profundity of their life together.

Paul's letter can still challenge us today. Indeed, when we realize that Paul was never a spokesperson for the status quo, but rather a utopian thinker, who believed that Israel's universal hope had come about in a way that no one could have imagined, then we can begin to see the strategy of his metaphors and rhetoric. In Galatians we find a constant inductive approach, reminding his listeners of the depths of their experience. He twists and turns cultural and religious icons on their heads in an effort to get his audience to recognize the reality and power of their life of transcendence. How do we understand and evaluate our experience? What would we add to the depths of our lives? What insurance policies do we constantly desire for our life in the Spirit? Are we not afraid to accept the reality of our freedom? Our older brother Paul asks from afar when are we going to grow up. Shall we finally stand on our own two feet and walk into God's future? Can we grasp that the life of transcendence is open to all on this planet and without it we shall not survive?

HEBREWS 11:8, 11-12, 17-19

The selected verses from Hebrews (for the context of Hebrews please see the second lesson for Christmas Day above) come from an encomium on faith (Heb. 11:1-40). Here faith is praised through a succession of examples drawn from the history of Israel. While there is no attempt to give an exhaustive definition to "faith" by the writer, the preliminary remarks (vv. 1-3) and the moving illustrations deliver a basis of motivation for the community.

This material provides a survival guide to the audience. Faith emerges as the *sine qua non*, the wherewithal to embark on life's journey. Faith is understood as the expectant quality and substance of human life. From faith's perspective one can gain, despite evidence to the contrary, a sense of how things fit together. As each example is brought forth, one can begin to confirm the illustration by seeing "in faith" how such was so. The words thus would provoke (and echo) the audience's own hopeful response, as each figure speaks to their condition. Such a rhetorical technique can be quite suggestive to the modern preacher. Can the preacher find those examples and models that enable people to visualize the hidden depths of their life of faith?

Verse 8, the opening to the subsection on the figures of Abraham and Sarah, focuses attention upon the risk of Abraham, who responded to God's call, despite the fact he did not know where he was going. Over the centuries many people have rightly used this verse as a fundamental example of faith. Verses 11-12 continue the saga of Abraham, who achieves the impossible through a stance of faith. (It should be noted that some manuscripts read "By faith Sarah herself, though barren, received power to conceive, even when she was too old, because she considered him faithful who had promised" [NRSV]. Such a reading is not impossible. Verse 35 brings in "women"; on the other hand, v. 12 returns the focus to Abraham.) Verses 17-19 resume the chapter's catalog of virtue. Behind these verses is the story of the *Aqedah*, that is, the binding of Isaac (Genesis 22). The horrible dimensions of the primitive story are foreshortened by the confident angle of faith (with even the note of resurrection, v. 19). In each of these brief episodes can we hear more than "twice-told tales"? Does God's word still speak through them to us? Are our lives built upon such invisible means of support?

COLOSSIANS 3:12-17

Our selection from Colossians is part of an extended parenetic passage (3:1—4:6). If one were to read the verses for today's lesson without considering both the proximate and remote contexts of the material, there would probably be few unfamiliar sounds. The various exhortations seem quite fitting even for a modern congregation. Yet, this apparent suitability may well be the result of a strenuous attempt by the writer of Colossians to influence the direction of the Christian movement.

Much ink has been spilt over the authorship and historical situation of the letter to the Colossians. While there is still some contention that Paul is the author of Colossians, a preponderance of critical observations leads to the conclusion that this letter was written by a disciple of Paul who wanted to maintain the apostle's authority as the church entered a new era. In comparison with the undisputed letters of Paul, one can detect differences in style and vocabulary, the omission of central Pauline themes, the greater use of traditional materials, the presence of new or significantly developed ideas, and indications of a church becoming more socially institutionalized.

Written ostensibly to the community at Colossae, a center of trade located in the Phrygian valley of the Lycus River, the letter takes great pains to present a christocentric interpretation of the community's experience. Such a position revises what appears to be a long-standing religious tendency in that region of Asia Minor. From the third century B.C.E. into the second century C.E. Phrygia was the site of numerous syncretistic movements. Evidently there was a traditional openness to blending various religious elements in order to participate in transcendent reality. Although one cannot be certain as to the exact nature of the crisis within Colossae, most scholars would agree that there has emerged a compelling blend of asceticism and moral rigorism, along with esoteric rites leading to visions and transcendent experience. The response to this by the author of Colossians is to claim that the community's life in Christ already is superior to any other form of knowledge and ritual, despite the persuasive presentation by the anonymous "teachers." In countering what would have been an attractive argument, the writer crafts a remarkable letter. First, he not only draws upon the authority of Paul but actually extends some of the basic Pauline strategies. By maintaining that the community already has the basis of genuine religious experience in Christ, the author continues the inductive Galatian argument. This position is strengthened by the enormous number of references to the community's liturgical and social life. To depart from this christological focus would mean, in effect, to deny their own experience. Moreover, the Colossians do not have to depart from their original experience in Christ to continue to mature and to experience the fullness of transcendence. Thus, by creatively merging Pauline and gnostic ideas, the author constructs a viable understanding of Christian existence for the community.

In our reading for today we find a concrete instance of this utilization of the Pauline strategy. As mentioned earlier, vv. 12-17 are part of a larger exhortation. It is important to consider the basis of this advice (3:1-4). Here the author goes beyond Paul's eschatological reservation to claim that the Christian already in the present enjoys the power of the resurrected life. While there is some muting of this claim in vv. 3-4, the fundamental direction has been set both in vv. 1-2 and elsewhere in Colossians. Already the community has been "clothed" with the "new self" and "renewed in knowledge" (3:10). This clothing metaphor continues in our section for today (vv. 12, 14). What is essential to see is that the various virtues urged (culminating with "love that binds all in perfection") build up the interdependence of the community (vv. 12-15). The various liturgical actions and rites are also for this upbuilding of the community (v. 16). Once more a Pauline idea (Paul's sole criterion for communal life) comes into play. Interdependence, not individual transcendence, characterizes the way in which the community express the eucharistic cycle of life (v. 17).

Our lesson for today, then, does not call for mere repetition. It presents an occasion to ask, What is the basis of our life together? How do we in our social and liturgical situations focus upon the fundamental character of our religious experience? Has the knowledge that we live in the power of the Risen One touched the concrete aspects of our existence?

GOSPEL: LUKE 2:22-40; JOHN 1:1-18

(For commentary on John 1:1-18 please see the Gospel for Christmas Day, above.)

LUKE 2:22-40

Today's passage forms a fitting conclusion to the entire infancy narrative of Luke. Just as the narrative begins with a story of a man and a woman in the Temple, so it ends with a man and a woman in the Temple. Luke, however, is doing more than merely balancing his narrative with this selection; he is once again injecting a note of universalism and challenge into what would otherwise be an ordinary story of religious duty.

This passage can be broken into four parts: vv. 22-24, the setting; vv. 25-35, the greeting of Simeon and his double oracle; vv. 36-38, the greeting of Anna; vv. 39 and 40, the conclusion. Interestingly, the ostensible reasons for journeying to Jerusalem—the purification of Mary and the presentation of the child in the Temple—are neglected in the passage. Although the two customs are mentioned, it seems, from vv. 22-24, that Luke has mainly in mind the rite of purification (see Lev. 12:1ff.). In any event, the main function of the opening verses is to place parents and child on the scene with Simeon.

Behind the composition of this entire passage is the story of Samuel (see 1 Samuel 1 and 2). There, too, parents bring their first-born to a holy place where an aged man blesses the parents. Luke, however, has added a number of ingredients to this pattern. The figures of both Simeon and Anna are portrayed in terms of the 'Anawim, those people in Israel who have placed all hope in God. More specifically, their hope is directed to the coming Messiah, the focal point of Jewish dreams. Moreover, the reiteration of fulfilling the law, combined with the action of the Spirit upon Simeon, could well imply the fulfillment of both the Law and the Prophets in this child. Such a possibility is borne out by the double oracle of Simeon (vv. 29-32, 34b-35). Some scholars argue that the first oracle, the *Nunc Dimittis*, is actually a secondary addition and that the story moves evenly from v. 27 to v. 34. If that is so, the addition of vv. 29-32 is another instance of the history of the Christian mission, which, having been rejected by many Jews, was accepted by the Gentiles. As it stands, the first oracle, taking much of its language from Isaiah (Isa. 40:5; 42:6; 46:13; 49:6; 52:9-10), foretells the proclamation to the Gentiles. Thus, incidentally, it parallels Matthew's magi scene. Unlike what we read in Isaiah, however, there is no notion here of subordinating the revelation to the Gentiles to the glory of Israel. The universalistic note one finds in Acts 15:14 and 28:28 is sounded here.

The second oracle, by contrast, sounds the note of division (see Luke 12:51-53) and scandal. The parenthetical clause, v. 35a, indicates that there is no guarantee for anyone, even the mother of Jesus: all must face the summons and challenge of the Gospel (see Luke 8:19-21). The true family of the Lukan Jesus is all who hear the Word and respond.

The third scene features the figure of Anna, who brings to mind the story of Judith. In a way, Anna is like those women in the time of Luke who held the office of widow (see 1 Tim. 5:3-16). Not only does her presence balance the opening Temple story with a closing Temple story, she gives another indication that not all will fail in discerning the child's identity.

A possible clue to the reading of today's Gospel is found in the double oracle of Simeon. Can we recite vv. 29-32 authentically today? To do so, we must first deal with the scandal of vv. 34b-35; for to be related to the Christ is to accept the sign of contradiction in the very fabric of one's life. Scholars and preachers who, by romanticizing the Holy Family, overlook this reality of faith do an injustice to the truth of the text.

In addition, the image of these two elderly characters challenges the modern reader. Presented as living on the margin, they have not grown old with the sense of desolation which afflicts many of us in the late twentieth century. This leads us to ask what is it that would permit such a vitality even at the edge of life. According to Luke "the Spirit was upon" Simeon. We can gather what Luke understands by the Spirit from the oracular utterances of Simeon. It is the Spirit who continues to open wide to the saving presence of God. At the same time, the decisive aspect of the Spirit makes itself felt, particularly in regard to the recognition of the child in question. In other words, in contrast to many of our contemporary assumptions, the deepest movement of human hope can continue to widen and to refine as we grow older. This growth inward comes about through a constant surrender in trust to the One who stirs such depths. In effect, Simeon's opening blessing is a summation of his entire life. There is also something more. One could even term it a certain "savoring." As one moves through life one acquires different, more refined, tastes. The most refined taste is that of sensing the fulfillment of one's deepest dreams. It is no longer the fresh and sharp pleasure of youth; rather, it is the patient appreciation of what has finally come about in God's good time.

The Name of Jesus
January 1

Lectionary	First Lesson	Psalm	Second Lesson	Gospel
Revised Common	Num. 6:22-27	Psalm 8	Gal. 4:4-7 *or* Phil. 2:5-13	Luke 2:15-21
Episcopal (BCP)	Exod. 34:1-8	Psalm 8	Rom. 1:1-7	Luke 2:15-21
Roman Catholic	Num. 6:22-27	Ps. 67:2-3, 5-6, 8	Gal. 4:4-7	Luke 2:16-21
Lutheran (LBW)	Num. 6:22-27	Psalm 8	Rom. 1:1-7 *or* Phil. 2:9-13 ·	Luke 2:21

FIRST LESSON: NUMBERS 6:22-27; EXODUS 34:1-8

NUMBERS 6:22-27

This ancient priestly benediction, well known to many modern Jewish and Christian congregations, probably was inserted into the book of Numbers during its exilic composition (587–538 B.C.E.). Thus, in a volume envisioning an address to each new generation as if standing on the edge of hope, at the border of the promised land, this blessing provides an assuring note of confidence.

Our reading follows the end of two sections concerned with the holiness and well-being of the community (Numbers 5–6) and precedes the enormous chap. 7, which details the offerings of the tribal leaders. With the sacred space cleared, as it were, the divine blessing is then delivered to be met with an overwhelming response. The priestly writer has provided a spectacle of hope for the exiles in Babylon, a pattern that can be renewed in the imagination and, perhaps, upon the return home. Significantly, most Scripture scholars point out that the blessing material is probably quite old. The editor has constructed a vivid scenario out of the debris of a desperate and damaged people.

The passage in itself is quite arresting. Verse 22 provides the narrative link to the surrounding material, while vv. 23 and 27 frame the blessing within the duties of the Aaronic priesthood. Most likely the blessing had been pronounced by priests over the congregation after the morning sacrifice in the Temple. Such would again be the case during the Second Temple Period (cf. Sir. 50:20ff.; Mishnah, *Tamid* 7.2). The blessing is a poetic gem in its own right. In the Hebrew one finds both formal parallelism and expansion in vv. 24-26. While there are only three words in v. 24, v. 25 continues with five, and v. 26 concludes with seven. In each of the three

lines the sacrosanct name Yahweh is the subject of both verbs. The content
of each line is also telling. Yahweh will bless and keep the people (v.
24), that is, provide them with prosperity, land, health, and the divine presence.
The favor of God is seen as the divine face "lighting" or "shining" on the
people (v. 25). Such a metaphor would be quite fitting if this were the
morning blessing in the Temple. There may also be some allusion to the
very "light" of creation (Gen. 1:3), implying that creation continues to happen as this blessing is spoken and received. In the final line Yahweh "lifts"
his face upon the people and gives them "shalom." "Shalom" embodies all
the blessings and favors expressed in the previous lines. It means that God
intends the total well-being of the people. This intent is reemphasized in v.
27 by the phrase "put my name on the Israelites." To "lay God's name on
them" means that the very selfhood of God is conveyed. All of the gifts
mentioned express the personal relation and fidelity of Yahweh to Israel.

In brief, this blessing delivers the best of God to Israel. At a time when
the people may well have questioned their very right to exist, the editor of
Numbers remembers this blessing that affirms the fundamental relation of
God to the people. If they were to live out of this blessing, realizing that
they were recognized and cared for by Yahweh, then they truly could continue not just to exist but to thrive. God wants nothing but their well-
being. Such a simple passage is staggering today. Quite often we think we
know what God wants of us. Perhaps even more often we know what God
wants of others. Yet does not this certainty mask our own desperation?
How few of us risk finding out that God wants nothing more, nor less,
than our selves?

EXODUS 34:1-8

Our reading for today from Exodus presupposes the graphic story of the
golden calf, the breaking of the tablets of the covenant by Moses, and the
people's punishment and repentance (chap. 32). Although that chaotic
scene has been fixed in many minds as coming from the time of Moses (an
example of which is found in De Mille's simplistic movie *The Ten Com-
mandments*), biblical scholars have long pointed out that this dramatic inci-
dent was probably a later construction influenced greatly by the northern
prophetic tradition. What appears in Exodus 32 is a concentrated criticism
of the fusion of Canaanite fertility rites with Yahwist worship.

Turning to Exod. 34:1-8 we can see further indications of editorial activity. Exodus 34:1-28 actually presents a covenantal tradition (vv. 2-5) that is
earlier than and distinct from the well-known Exodus 20. Many scholars
would join the material from Exodus 34 with the earlier portions of Exodus
19. What has happened, of course, is that the compiler of Exodus has dis-
placed the older Yahwist tradition of the covenant with the Elohist rendering

(Exodus 20). Further, the Yahwist material is turned nicely into a covenant renewal scene in Exodus 34 by inserting the note of "former tablets" (vv. 1, 4) along with a traditional cultic confession (vv. 6-7; cf. Num. 14:18; Neh. 9:17, 31; Ps. 103:8; Jer. 32:18; Jon. 4:2). Likewise, Exod. 34:1 finds its setting in the tent of meeting (Exod. 33:7), an ancient tent-shrine that functioned as a place of meeting and oracles. Verse 8 provides a response to the theophany in vv. 5-6 as well as a transition to the petition for forgiveness (v. 9), coming just before the covenant itself (vv. 10-26).

This revision is not a calculated manipulation. Rather, the revision comes out of the long and difficult experience of the people of Israel. By the time the scroll of Exodus was undergoing the priestly revision in the sixth century both the prophetic witness from the ninth century and the period of the Babylonian exile had taught a hard lesson: the people continually failed to live up to their part of the relationship with Yahweh. However, this revision was not written out of despair; instead, it signaled the possibility of renewal. Thus, the greatly transmuted original scene continues to suggest dramatic possibility. This mythic stage is, however, not simply the momentous beginning of Israel's story but the occasion for abiding renewal. Israel can begin again and again according to the promise of this version.

Many modern Bible readers and pastors are not overly excited by peeling away the various layers of biblical traditions. Indeed, determining who said what appears no more than an esoteric detective game. Yet, there is more at stake than an academic exercise. Whenever we avoid these critical issues, we are being unfair both to ourselves and to our ancestors in faith, for we refuse to see the complexity and depths of our lives. Today's story does not come down to us untouched. This is more than a twice-told tale. It comes out of repeated failures of fidelity and nerve. Yet the storyteller returns to the campsite in the desert to experience once again "The LORD" (v. 5). The story has been handed down in confidence that the Lord will "pass by" in those ancient cultic words (vv. 6-7). Despite the disasters of the past, reaching into the present situation, the writer returns with Moses to the mountain with those two blank tablets, hoping that there will be words once more for his people.

As the passage ends in a quiet, reverent response, we are left with the task of retelling this story once again. If this story truly works, it is because we have begun to remember those moments when our lives have been complicated and deepened by God's mystery. But how often have we forgotten those "peak moments," those intimations of genuine life? Can we return in our brokenness, in remembrance, and in hope? Can we listen to someone other than ourselves? Can we be surprised yet again by a love that refuses to stay away from us?

SECOND LESSON: ROMANS 1:1-7; GALATIANS 4:4-7; PHILIPPIANS 2:5-13

(For Gal. 4:4-7 see the comments on the second lesson for the First Sunday after Christmas, above.)

ROMANS 1:1-7

The beginning verses of Romans are markedly distinct from the other Pauline letter openings (1 Cor. 1:1-3; 2 Cor. 1:1-2; Phil. 1:1-2; Phlm. 1-3; 1 Thess. 1:1.). Not even Gal. 1:1-5 can compete with this expanded format. It is not sufficient to say that this formal introduction is simply due to Paul's unfamiliarity with his audience. On the contrary, the destination of this letter has greatly factored into Paul's rhetorical entrance. Too often people read Romans as a theological tract without any sense of time or place. Romans cannot be understood without recognizing the basic theological competitor for Paul: Roman imperial theology. His audience would have been quite accustomed to the gospel of the Caesars. In these opening lines Paul enters the lists against the good news that universal peace was achieved by the miracle of Actium and sustained by the imperial might and law.

A close reading of the material brings out Paul's remarkable stance. First, the basic opening formula of a letter writer sending greetings to an addressee can be detected in the first and last verses of today's lesson (vv. 1, 7). Many scholars have pointed out the probable pre-Pauline creedal formula in vv. 3b-4 ("who was descended . . . resurrection from the dead"). Verse 3b may well come from an early messianic understanding of Jesus (cf. 2 Sam. 7:11b-16, the first lesson for the Fourth Sunday of Advent, above), while v. 4 emerges from the early believers' reinterpretation of Pss. 2:7 and 110:1. These two distinct versions of the fate of Jesus had already been joined before Paul employed them. Additionally, many have noted how Paul includes his new audience in the universal scope of the Gentile mission (v. 6). It is sometimes further argued that the royal references (the messianic descent from David in v. 3b, and the enthronement of "the Son of God" in v. 4) add weight and authority to Paul's mission (v. 5a, "through whom we have received benefit and mission" [NRSV: grace and apostleship]).

Yet such observations by themselves are too short-sighted for this passage. The pre-Pauline creedal fragments (vv. 3b-4) fill out part of Paul's description of the "gospel of God" (v. 1). Verse 2 indicates that this "announcement" had been promised through the Jewish prophetic writings. In his official capacity of "slave of Jesus Christ," Paul serves as a designated "legate" (*apostolos*) for the good news (v. 1). "Gospel" does not refer to any written document; rather, here it is an oral proclamation of matters of import (cf. Rom. 1:16, "gospel" as powerful communication). In effect, then, the voices of the prophets come together with early Christian formulations to embody the gospel in Paul's address to the Roman communities. The rhetorical effect of such formal remarks resounds in vv. 5-6 where Paul reiterates his mission and brings his audience into its range. Indeed, Paul's mission is twofold. It is for the announcement of the good news (v. 1, *eis euaggelion*) and for the response of faith/trust (v. 5, *eis upakoen pisteos*, a "trustful response"). In other words, Paul's universal mission is to proclaim a message that will receive a trusting response (not a "submission in faith" as some translate, thereby exposing their political assumptions).

Paul's opening words become a major gambit when one begins to fill in the political nuances of his language. Already the imperial "gospel" has been mentioned. Such a term was used to spread the propaganda of the imperial success story. "Peace and prosperity" (*eirene, charis*, v. 7b) was a standard political cliche. Even the notion of Paul as a "slave" and "delegate" can mirror the imperial bureaucracy. Of course, the messianic allusion in v. 3b and the enthronement scene in v. 4 present a direct contender to the imperial office. The phrase "son of God" also was common currency. Finally, "faith"/"trust" (*pistis*) reflects the prized Roman virtue of *pietas* without which the entire Roman dream falls apart. Thus, one can say that Paul's introduction plays with some of the most deeply embedded dreams of the Roman empire. His "gospel" stands up against the "gospel" that rules the civilized world. As he proclaims a message about a sovereign who effectively distributes favors to the entire world, Paul invites his Roman audience to join in this universal movement.

As the rest of Romans goes on, one can see that this new sovereignty is found not in obedience to the will of law but in obedience to human vulnerability and weakness. A new world is envisioned, no longer along the lines of the hegemony of authority but in terms of partnership. Salvation now is opposed to power and authority (to which the Roman theology of peace was dedicated). Of course, the lasting irony is that Paul the rebel long has been silenced. Not only did he meet his fate in the center of the power structure he opposed but he has been embalmed in later ecclesiastical winding sheets.

PHILIPPIANS 2:5-13

Our second lesson from Philippians brings before us one of the most commented upon passages in the history of interpretation. Today's selection (2:5-13) is actually part of a larger exhortatory section in the letter to the Philippians. Evidently the letter was written by Paul during an imprisonment (1:13). While the letter has been assigned traditionally to the time of Paul's confinement in Rome, more recent scholarship suggests more probably the period of incarceration at Ephesus or (less likely) at Jerusalem. Nor is it clear as to the specific occasion for writing the letter. There may well have been some difficulty within the community or even the threat of outside trouble (1:30). Acts 16:12-40 may provide some of the troubled background for the letter. Nevertheless, the main point of this letter is clear: to assist the building up of the "partnership" (*koinonia*) of the Philippians in the face of continued struggle and growth.

In turning to the second lesson for today, one can detect some clues. Due to the non-Pauline language found in vv. 6-11, the introductory remark of v. 5, and the concluding connection of v. 12 ("Therefore, my beloved, . . ."), one can easily remove this material from the surrounding exhortatory remarks (vv. 5, 12-13). Yet, although vv. 6-11 can be isolated as a pre-Pauline hymn (vv. 10, 11, "every knee should bend," "every tongue confess" suggest liturgical actions), numerous debates have been launched over the source, background, structure, redaction, and meaning of the piece. Space does not permit an exposition of the various backgrounds argued for the hymn. The Jewish Wisdom tradition (e.g., Proverbs 8–9) may well be the crucible for this material. Indeed, others have suggested more specifically that the suffering servant theme from Second Isaiah or that of the vindication of the suffering righteous one (Wisdom of Solomon 2–5) may well be the basis for this hymn. Finally, the redeemer myth found throughout the ancient world is also a candidate for providing the imaginative matrix for this piece.

What has often been overlooked in searching for the imaginative realm of this hymn is the propaganda surrounding the character of Alexander the Great. In Plutarch's *On the Fortune of Alexander* 1.8 (330D), Alexander is described as a conqueror quite distinct from all others. "He did not overrun Asia like a thief . . . nor did he consider it something to plunder. . . ." "Because he wanted to show that all things on earth were subject to one principle and one government, that all humans were one people, he conformed himself in such a way." Only his untimely death prevented this utopian vision from becoming a reality. Three points should be made. First, there are telling linguistic similarities between the Philippian hymn and Plutarch's treatment of Alexander. Second, one cannot overlook the historical background of Philippi. Originally named after the father of Alexander the Great, the city was settled by Roman veterans of the Civil Wars and rebuilt in the splendors of Roman fashion. Third, this dream of a civilized society, brought about through the agency of a divine man, remained alive in the Roman propaganda machine. The emperors exploited this lingering hope. It would not be unlikely, therefore, that the legendary drive of Alexander the Great was refined and revised through the wisdom speculation of the early Jesus believers.

But there is more than just a matter of comparison. If Paul has added "that is, death on a cross" to v. 8, then an enormous step has been taken. First, it should be recalled that in the ancient world the divine realm usually stopped at the threshold of death. Second, one could actually read vv. 6-8 (minus Paul's addition) as referring to a divine figure taking on the appearance of humanity but not really entering fully into the depths of human experience. Both points reinforce the other. Just as a divine redeemer "touches down" only to return unscathed to the heavenly realm, so too could this figure of the hymn. It seems that Paul has forced the issue by poignantly adding that this movement goes right into death, into the heart of human frailty and powerlessness. Exactly where Alexander's triumph halted, the path of Jesus penetrates. Here we find a figure who indiscriminately joins with all, renouncing his legal rights. And, precisely because of this complete identification with the depths of humanity, God sustains that nobody. Furthermore, the image of God itself is transformed, since God no longer is imagined supporting the sovereign elite. Rather, because God confirms this "Jesus," the Philippians can discover how genuine authority works—in solidarity with the nameless ones. Finally, the additional advice in vv. 12-13 maintains this vision. The human struggle itself is the locus of the divine presence. There is no need other than to enter human life with a profound sense of compassion and sympathy (cf. 2:1).

GOSPEL: LUKE 2:15-21

The Gospel reading for today takes its cue primarily from a series of literary echoes. First, the passage completes the three-part scenario of Luke 2:1-20. The participants of scene one (vv. 1-7) confront those of scene two (vv. 8-15). More particularly, v. 16 links the angelic annunciation with the child in the manger (vv. 7, 12), while vv. 17-18, 20 confirm the angel's message. This, in turn, leads to further action, whereby the shepherds make known what has happened and glorify God.

Perhaps most startling in this narrative action is the silent pondering of Mary (v. 19). In a certain sense, this verse stands off by itself, interrupting the rush of the shepherds. We need to consider the contrast between Mary and the shepherds. For the latter characters the angelic words have been confirmed by what they have witnessed. They then turn to reporting what has happened to them. Mary, on the other hand, keeps a silent vigil, "turning these words over in her heart."

What is crucial for understanding this Lukan material is that the phrase "these words" touch on the Lukan understanding of discipleship. The one who genuinely keeps the words of God and brings forth fruit in patience (Luke 8:15; 11:28) is the true disciple. In other words, the discerning of what has happened is not resolved by some quick conclusion; on the contrary, the disciple must resist this temptation. If one reads all of Luke then one comes to realize that one should not close off interpretation until the power of the resurrection becomes manifest (cf. Luke 24:13-32). This means that one cannot understand fully the career and fate of Jesus until one has taken in, or better, been taken in by, the power of the Spirit, issuing from the resurrection. Another way of putting this is that only through the backward glance of faith do the events of the Christian story take their shape and meaning. Thus, even in the heart of the Christmas season, the resurrection shines through!

In light of such thematic points, the verse describing Mary becomes rather singular. It is not, then, some mere report of her humility. Rather, it provides the reader with a basic reflection of the way in which the Lukan community understood the task of discipleship. One needs to "turn over" events in one's life to see how they ultimately touch on the Spirit of the resurrection. This "turning things over" is no small matter, for it challenges us all to go beyond our ideas or images of resurrection and to discover whether the resurrection is genuinely at work in our lives.

There is a further underlying assumption to this verse in the understanding of the Lukan community. They were of the conviction that the Spirit had not come and gone but remained ever present to help them deal with their reflections. Certainly the contemporary theological phrase "discerning the signs of the times" is an heir to this position. It should be further pointed out that such a stance does not leave everything up to some divine final solution; on the contrary, it demonstrates how disciples are summoned to ponder the depths of their lives and to discover eventually the movement of the Spirit in their experience.

Verse 19, then, stands both in juxtaposition to the action of the shepherds and in anticipation of further happenings. This seemingly neutral description is actually theological dynamite. For it leaves open to all who would consider the thought that our experience is unfinished, that the future seeds of our present life are still waiting to be opened. It means that for both activist and contemplative God is on the move and that this movement can only be detected by those willing to wait and sense this momentum. In short, the echoes that we can pick up with this verse and its immediate surrounding material as well as with that of the entire Gospel can lead us to perceive further reverberations in our own lives. To be sure, unless one can come to this level of "sensing" this material, the story has made no genuine contact. The shepherds might come and go; but the silent witness remains for more.

Finally, it should be noted that the last verse of today's reading functions as either an appended remark to vv. 1-20 or as a narrative hinge to the following purification scene (vv. 22ff.). It is interesting that the circumcision does not have the dramatic size of John the Baptizer's elaborate scene (1:59ff.). Rather, it confirms yet again another angelic message (1:31). The echoes increase.

Second Sunday after Christmas

Lectionary	First Lesson	Psalm	Second Lesson	Gospel
Revised Common	Jer. 31:7-14 or Sir. 24:1-12	Ps. 147:12-20 or Wisd. 10:15-21	Eph. 1:3-14	John 1:(1-9), 10-18
Episcopal (BCP)	Jer. 31:7-14	Psalm 84	Eph. 1:3-6, 15-19a	Matt. 2:13-15, 19-23 or Luke 2:41-52
Roman Catholic	Sir. 24:1-2, 8-12	Ps. 147:12-15, 19-20	Eph. 1:3-6, 15-18	John 1:1-18
Lutheran (LBW)	Isa. 61:10—62:3	Ps. 147:13-21	Eph. 1:3-6, 15-18	John 1:1-18

FIRST LESSON: ISAIAH 61:10—62:3; SIRACH 24:1-12; JEREMIAH 31:7-14

(For Isa. 61:10—62:3 see the first lesson for the First Sunday after Christmas, above.)

JEREMIAH 31:7-14

Today's reading from Jeremiah, a palimpsest of hope, comes from the part of Jeremiah known as the "Book of Consolation" (30:1—31:41). This title has been given to those two chapters due to the distinctive character of the material. In contrast to the oracular condemnations throughout the prophetic scroll, these chapters not only deliver a most encouraging vision but also speak to the long-demolished Northern Kingdom of Israel.

In attempting to resolve the placement of this material within the compositional history of the scroll of Jeremiah, scholars have hit upon a compelling explanation. It would seem that there were a series of oracles directed to the northern people by the young Jeremiah during the reign of Josiah of Judah. Although the Northern Kingdom had been occupied by Assyria for over a hundred years, the weakened Assyrian presence, brought about by the death of Ashurbanipal in 627 B.C.E., allowed King Josiah to attempt to extend the boundaries of Judah into the northern territory. From 2 Kings 23:4, 15 it can be seen that his religious reform reached Bethel. His death at the battle of Megiddo (2 Kings 23:29-30; 2 Chron. 35:20-24) against Neco the Pharaoh would also argue for such northern designs. Archaeological evidence would confirm such activity. Finally, pilgrimages by northerners to Jerusalem (31:12), a practice curtailed by the first Israelite ruler Jeroboam (1 Kings 12:26-33), actually resumed during the time of Jeremiah (41:4-5). It was during this window of political opportunity that the oracles to Israel may well have been constructed (30:5-7; 30:10-15; 30:18-21; 31:2-6; 31:7-14; 31:15-20; 31:21-22).

With the fall of Josiah (621 B.C.E.) and the eventual exile of Judah to Babylon, the northern oracles took on a different tone. As found with the present text of Jeremiah, the northern oracles have been placed within a more inclusive vision. Now both the northern and southern peoples are the beneficiaries of the revised material. The editorial frame (30:1-4; 31:1; 31:23-26), insertions (30:8-9; 30:16-17; 30:22; 30:23-24), and inclusion of new oracles (31:27-30; 31:31-37; 31:38-40) push the earlier poetry into a different context. The hope that was offered to Israel now comes to both ravaged peoples. It should not be overlooked that such hope was quite unheard of in the ancient world. A people carried off into exile was a people without an identity, a people on the edge of extinction. Such encouraging songs went against the harsh momentum of political history.

The verses for today present a bombast of hope. The nonexistent Northern Kingdom is addressed by name (vv. 7, 9, 10, 11). Yahweh alone will bring them back from the ends of the earth (v. 8). Those on the very margin of life ("the blind and the lame," women pregnant and in labor, v. 8b) will be included. The people of Israel will not be given up by God, who will redeem his "firstborn" (v. 9). The joyous reunion will turn into a glorious pilgrimage to Jerusalem (v. 12) where abundance and celebration will be the order of the new day.

Now we reread these lines today. How can these ancient sounds echo in our lives? Recall that these lines were not written without the recognition of a desperate reality. Indeed, they were saved by the editors of Jeremiah precisely because they could offer encouragement to people on the edge. Thus, it is incumbent upon us to ask about our condition. Where are those who are on the edge of extinction today? What parts of our world, our communities, even ourselves, are in critical condition? Do we believe that the God of our ancestors still calls out to those on the edge? Can we detect intimations of poetry in the trashy prose of today? Can we see a future breaking in where we would expect none? Shall we join in this unfinished dance?

SIRACH 24:1-12

This reading comes from Ben Sira's exalted hymn of Wisdom. Although only the first twelve verses have been selected, the entire chapter should be read to catch the rhetorical course of the hymn. Emerging from "highest heavens" (vv. 1-4), the progress of Wisdom moves "over every people and nation" (vv. 5-7) to a "dwelling in Jacob" (vv. 8-12). Here Wisdom graphically "takes root" and grows like a luxuriant tree (vv. 13-17), promising fulfillment for all who would experience her (vv. 19-22). In v. 23 it is stated that "all of this" is the Mosaic law, which overflows in insight like Eden's rivers, inundating everyone with its transcendent abundance (vv.

25-29). From vv. 30-34 we hear Ben Sira's personal commentary, attesting to this unending flow of Wisdom, which turns even his words into an inspired scroll for future generations.

It is crucial to situate this poetry within its historical context. Writing before 180 B.C.E., Ben Sira faced squarely the collision of two different cultures. The Hellenistic world was making serious inroads into Israel. Would Ben Sira, the teacher of Wisdom, reject the outside world that was now part of the commercial and social life of Jerusalem? Or, would he give into the pressures of an invading culture and abandon his traditions? The first option was fundamentally impractical and contrary to much of his experience. On the other hand, he refused to give up his heritage precisely because of his ability to find another response. Ben Sira brought the Hellenistic Wisdom tradition home, identifying the best of that tradition with Torah. Performing an intellectual *jujitsu*, Ben Sira turned the tables on this cultural invasion, as he claimed that the wisdom the world sought was to be found in the schools of Israel. In so doing, Ben Sira revised earlier Jewish Wisdom material (Proverbs 8–9), while disagreeing with the pessimistic voices of the multifaceted Jewish debate (such as 1 Enoch 42:1-2, where Wisdom cannot be found or Job 28 where no one but the Lord has access to Wisdom). Our reading for today, then, is a provocative poem, as Ben Sira throws down the cultural gauntlet. He not only retells the creation story (v. 3) but situates the universal aspect of Wisdom within the particular confines of Israel. The Mosaic tradition is not merely saved, it is expanded and given the very momentum of this worldwide movement.

But why is Ben Sira's response important beyond an historical footnote? Why should the modern Bible reader wonder about this majestic hymn? The ancient search for Wisdom was based upon a fundamental drive: the hope that somehow the universe made sense, that there was some inner consistency to experience, some connection to life. Moreover, the Wisdom tradition, both within and outside Judaism, assumed that whatever was learned from this human search could be passed on and tested through further experience. In brief, the Wisdom tradition profoundly challenges the modern age to take up this task, to go beyond the superficiality of our culture and to face the dread of our lives. Can we experience meaning at the depths of our lives? What connections do we sense at the edge of our existence? Can we find words to pass our hard-won Wisdom on to future generations? Has Wisdom found a home in us?

SECOND LESSON: EPHESIANS 1:3-19

Our second lesson for today is taken from the opening chapter of Ephesians. Unlike other letters bearing Paul's name, Ephesians is quite distinct. The style and language differ markedly from that found in the letters critically attributed to Paul. Further, the significant theological changes, the lack of specificity in regard to issues, places, and events, as well as the dependence of the letter upon earlier Pauline lines and the letter of the Colossians, argue strongly for late first-century authorship. The anonymous writer, possibly a Jew, attempted to bring forward the Pauline heritage to a new generation of Christians by calling them back to the foundation of their existence, to the gospel of Paul, and to the implications of their own baptism. The letter may have been written originally as a circular letter to the communities of Asia Minor. Eventually it seems to have been positioned as the introductory or cover letter to collections of letters attributed to Paul. In short, the very textual history of the letter provides clues to the developing history of the late first-century and early second-century Christian movement.

The passage for today can be broken into two parts (vv. 3-14, 15-19). Verses 3-14 in the Greek are actually one long sentence, a rhetorical conglomeration of clauses and phrases. The entire piece is a benediction, praising God for divine benefits and indirectly urging the listeners to continue to live out of such benefaction. As the phrases build one upon the other, a monumental result is achieved. Not only does one receive the impression that there is a fundamental unity of purpose to the cosmos, where God is the true actor, Christ the mediator of the divine benefits, and believers genuine participants in this universal design, but one is forced by the very back and forth focus of the clauses to go over and over the divine plan—yet each time with a different emphasis or nuance. The benediction is the verbal equivalent to Trajan's Column, where the entire narrative of the emperor's career was carved in spiraling fashion until one reaches the glorious statue of Trajan standing atop.

More specifically, we can see that v. 3 provides the basic downbeat to this cascade of praise. The God and Father of the Lord Jesus Christ is blessed for providing every "spiritual blessing" to us "in Christ." What follows in vv. 4-14 is a magnificent elaboration on this system of benefaction. In vv. 4-6 we see that this largesse had been planned from "before the foundation of the universe." The election and destiny as adopted children of God had been made so that believers could praise the One who had given so freely. Then, in vv. 7-10 the redemptive plan becomes clearly manifest through the blood of Christ and the revelation that this was the mysterious will of God to "gather all things up" in Christ. Through vv. 11-12 the future implications of this design are noted, while vv. 13-14 bring the listeners directly into this scheme. If, as some scholars suspect, the author was drawing on language from the baptismal rites of the time, then the phrases through this extended sentence would constantly speak to the experience of the listening congregations.

Verses 15-19 are taken from the next major portion of Ephesians (1:15-23). In fact, vv. 15-19 also are one long sentence in the Greek. Here the author draws on the predictable thanksgiving format found in the typical Pauline letter. Verse 15 allows the figure of Paul to connect with a new generation of believers. Notice the intriguing prayer that the listeners receive a "spirit of wisdom and revelation" so that the "eyes of the heart might be enlightened (v. 18). Three indirect questions serve as the object of such knowledge. They are to know "what is the hope," "what are the riches," and "what is the power" (vv. 18-19) to which they are called. This is clarified in vv. 20-23, which point out that the power of God is now resident in the resurrected Christ who rules over all and fills out the body of the church.

This portion of Ephesians is remarkable. At a time when the empire was enjoying economic success and reaching its farthest territorial limits, a religious minority, considered socially deviant at best, attempted to work out alternative building plans for the universe. Such a document raises numerous questions for the modern believer. How deep is our vision, how profound our confidence? Do we really believe that all things hold together? Or, have our experiences of alienation and fragmentation detonated this possibility? Has the invisible hand of the marketplace replaced the merciful mystery of God's will? Has the violence of this century drained away the hope of our redemption?

GOSPEL: JOHN 1:1-18; MATTHEW 2:13-15, 19-23

(For commentary on John 1:1-18 see the Gospel for Christmas Day, above.)

Our reading from Matthew today is a history of Israel in miniature. Especially if we restore vv. 16-18 to our passage, we shall find echoes of the tales of the young Moses found in and outside of the Bible. Just as Moses narrowly escaped so now Jesus. Further, does not Joseph recall the earlier Joseph, the man of dreams? And, from a broader angle, one could say that Matthew would have this vignette from the early life of Jesus recapitulate the entire life of Israel. The sojourn in Egypt, the exile and the return may well coincide with vv. 13-15, vv. 16-18, and vv. 19-23 respectively. The early travels of Jesus would thus be reiterations of his people's displacements.

Today's selection also contains two more specific dream-appearance sequences (vv. 13b-15a and 19-21). They are certainly less worked over than the one in Matt. 1:20-24. After the introductory v. 13a, which joins the preceding story of the Magi, there follow the dream appearance to Joseph, the command to flee, and Joseph's obedient response. Verse 15b presents a Matthaean deepening of the meaning by his citation from Hosea 11:1. This verse could easily have been placed after the return from Egypt. So why is it here? Before answering this question, we should point out that the next section makes use once more of the dream-appearance format, which apparently is continued in vv. 22 and 23. It is questionable why the angelic messenger did not forewarn Joseph about the entire situation all at once. Does it have anything to do with the citation in v. 23?

In order to place this passage in perspective, we must note that today's reading omits vv. 16-18, which speak of the massacre of the innocents. It has been suggested by numerous scholars that the infancy narrative of Matthew has certain motifs that cast the early life of Jesus in the light of the stories of young Moses. Moses also was persecuted and had a narrow escape. In some later versions of the life of Moses, his father was even sent a dream warning of the imminent danger to the child. Indeed, the words "those who had designs on the life of the child are dead" more than echo Exod. 4:19. Furthermore, Joseph, the father of Jesus, can be seen in the light of Joseph the patriarch, a man of dreams who was responsible for bringing his family into Egypt.

We can look at today's passage from an even larger perspective. Verses 13-15 coincide with Israel's sojourn in Egypt. Verses 16-18, particularly v. 18, allude to the exile. Finally, vv. 19-23 deal not only with the return to Israel but with the return to Nazareth. Matthew is interested in showing that the early life of Jesus recapitulates the entire history of Israel. Just as his genealogy can be traced from Abraham, so can his early travels be tied to the displacements of his people.

Matthew's concern for Nazareth poses some questions. It is significant that Luke had no problem about Jesus' being from Nazareth. His problem was getting Mary and Joseph to Bethlehem! For Matthew, on the other hand, the question was reversed. Since they were already residents of Bethlehem (2:11), the problem was how to get them to Nazareth. Matthew does this in two ways: he uses an angelic dream, and he finds the Scripture that this movement fulfills (v. 23). There are a number of difficulties with v. 23. Does it simply mean that Jesus was from the town of Nazareth? To reduce the meaning to this alone would overlook some possibilities upon which the term *Nazoraios* plays. The word *nazir* refers to a holy one who has been dedicated to God from birth (see Judg. 16:17, Isa. 4:3). And the word *neser* means the Messianic branch from the shoot of David (Isa. 11:1ff.). Either or both references could have been in Matthew's mind, for he might have made the easy connection with the Emmanuel prediction (1:25). Thus, not only does this allusion give a sense of fulfillment to

Jesus' geographical location, it also ties in many themes that Matthew is working on in his Gospel.

There is something more here. Matthew not only reiterates the past but gives it a certain direction. The sense of fulfillment, noted in the scriptural citations, indicates that something is afoot, that there is some advance into what has been dearly desired. A purposefulness, then, characterizes this narrative. From such a perspective a universal missionary effort would become possible.

But how can this passage enter into our time? Before we too quickly "spiritualize" the meaning of this passage, let us remember that Matthew identifies Jesus with the historical journey of his people. In light of that, let us continue in Matthew's momentum by taking seriously the enormous memory of the Shoah, and by listening to the hopes that enliven Jewish life today. In short, a way into our Gospel may very well come from recapitulating the contemporary story of the Jews. We may well learn anew what it means to dream in the face of terror. And we may also wonder how often we have been playing Herod's part! Furthermore, we may well begin to see that this story is an old one—of children at risk, of parents getting out in the nick of time through some unexpected intervention. As we read the daily stories in our newspapers and see the stunned eyes of the innocents in Africa and in the former Yugoslavia we find the story coming hauntingly alive again. Yes, it is an old story, a human one, about which we forget and do nothing at our own peril.